COSMIC JOURNEYS
OF THE
ALICHINA WASI

-
-
-
-
-
-

MICHAEL ZEFF

Copyright © 2021 by Michael Zeff

Cover Art, Editing, and Formatting by Michael Zeff
Type Set in Hoefler Text

Excerpts from *Tao Te Ching* by Stephen Mitchell
Copyright © Stephen Mitchell

All Rights Reserved. No part of this book may be reproduced or used in any manner without written permission of the copyright owner.

*To the beating heart, to the shining sun,
to the eye of All as One.*

Contents

INTRODUCTION		i
	The Call	v
	An Indigenous Perspective	xiii
	The Approach	xix
JOURNEY ONE	The Mind	01
JOURNEY TWO	Portals of Form	05
JOURNEY THREE	The Council of Duality	23
JOURNEY FOUR	By the Wings of Humanity	37
JOURNEY FIVE	Ego's Waiting Room	51
FIRELIGHT CEREMONY I	Vibration & Fractal Dimensions	63
JOURNEY SIX	Informal Operation	71
INTERLUDE	Unlimited Energy	77
JOURNEY SEVEN	A Vision, A Dream	81
JOURNEY EIGHT	Fear, Myself, & I	87
FIRELIGHT CEREMONY II	Listening	93
JOURNEY NINE	The Ocean	97
FIRELIGHT CEREMONY III	What Shines the Sun	101
JOURNEY TEN	Grandmother's Blessing	107
INTEGRATION		111

Introduction

Cos • mos *(noun)* Harmony, order (as of an integral body or self-inclusive system); *Antonym:* chaos

One may neither anticipate nor directly pursue awareness of a cosmic nature; just as one may neither anticipate nor directly pursue a color one's eye cannot see.

For this, the expansion of perception is key. With tremendous willingness and surrender, one may cleanse the lens of perception to peer through an open aperture unfiltered. By releasing all constraints of thought, identification, physicality, and spirituality, one may integrate the underlying essence of *cosmos* within oneself by way of the spontaneous journey. Within this is the amalgamation of *cosmos* and *chaos*—for, true to the paradox of life, both are facets of one integral whole.

This book is born of a serendipitous two-year-long study into the nature of reality in a tiny village in a strange land. I found myself engulfed in intensive yogic and meditative practices every day for nearly 600 days. During this time I was asked to participate in indigenous healing arts and ceremonies guided by shamans who had developed lifelong relationships with the spirit of a sacred plant medicine, Ayahuasca.

In this book, I share journeys for which I alone did not beckon, but which arose within me during ceremonies held with great reverence and respect for the powerful plant spirits with whom I connected, and through whom I received invaluable guidance along the way.

My intention here is to share the experiences, rather than the myriad of extrapolations and interpretations which inevitably arise through years of integration and reflection. I still marvel at the inherent implications of these journeys, as they defy the threshold of any conceptual understanding I alone could have conjured.

In reading, you are invited to freely accept or deny anything expressed herein. I do invite you to consider one perspective: that the rational brain-mind is not qualified to claim a whole understanding of these journeys in and of itself. Attempts to condense the underlying essence of these journeys into the narrow confines of the mind may be willfully surrendered, as this mode of interpretation alone may obscure that which exists both prior to and beyond the scope of human cognition. Like attempting to cook an egg with a hammer, other tools are required. We each bear these innate faculties—when one chooses to step back from the mind, they arise in the space created.

Each journey may be seen as a finger pointing toward a star in the night sky. One has the option to merely gaze at the finger, or one may turn keenly perceptive eyes upon the immensity toward which the finger points—and with clear intention, go there.

Some of the journeys I experienced are not included in this book—those that are, are presented in chronological order. Some were so deeply enmeshed in personal experiences that they are not to be included here; others involved content which remains incommunicable or unclear; other ceremonies—including some in which a

INTRODUCTION

much larger volume of Ayahuasca was ingested—were spent simply sitting silently in the *Alichina Wasi* for many hours, with only an underlying awareness of the medicine coursing through the body. Ayahuasca affects consciousness on far subtler levels than that of journeys and cosmic visions.

In addition to journeys in the presence of Ayahuasca, included in these writings are journeys with psilocybin. Though psilocybin is often abused as a recreational psychedelic, indigenous cultures understand that these mushroom bodies are hosts of powerful spirits. When approached with respectful humility and openness within the safe container of ceremony, they may help guide one beyond the limited scope of human experience and expand the illusory bounds of perception ad infinitum.

Throughout these pages, excerpts of my original journal entries are included in italics. A few of these have been lightly edited for grammatical clarification or to omit names, and are otherwise presented as-written either during or a few hours after each journey.

Because I had no clue that this book would come to exist as these journeys unfolded, the journal entries written amidst these experiences provide a sort of grounding time-stamp, a layer of vulnerability in the innocence and honesty of words written to myself, for myself, by my Self.

Simply, I did not anticipate any of this.

The Call

Glistening beams of light refracted through shallow Pacific water. I reached down toward warbly emerald-tinted sand to unstrap my surfboard leash and grabbed the quivering tail fin of a fish instead.

Perplexities abound upon the coast of Ecuador. Prior to arrival in this magical land, I was briefly situated at a rather antiquitous ranch in the western foothills of California's Sierra Nevada mountains.

While I harvested apples on that beautiful autumn hillside, the mother of a cohabitant visited for a week. We spoke at length about travels, about the many colorful cultures of Earth. I mentioned a bizarre trip to Ecuador three years prior, during which my exceptionally modest bank account was remotely drained by a hacker in the US.

"Where were you going in Ecuador?" she asked, with keen interest.

"To the coast; but I didn't quite make it," I admitted, somewhat reluctantly.

"Do you plan to go again sometime?"

I was surprised by her expression. "I have no plans, but anything is possible."

She leaned back with a smirk only worn by those with the cumulative wisdom of many ages. "My husband and I have a house on the coast of Ecuador."

At the end of their visit, I was asked to look after their home in Ecuador in the coming spring. I said yes and booked the cheapest flight I could find.

On the morning of departure from the Sierra Nevada mountains, while my imagination reeled with sights of Ecuador's lush seaside jungles, I dug my station wagon out of two feet of snow, plowed the icy quarter-mile driveway with an old jimmy-rigged tractor, spontaneously sold my car en-route to the airport, and sat patiently waiting for the boarding call. Though I had visited Ecuador once before, I had no way to conceive of what was to come.

After navigating layovers, terminals, busses and taxis in elementary Spanish, I awoke to bright flowers, fresh ocean air, and coconut palms set upon the backdrop of a glimmering pastel sky. I heard a neighbor calling through the door of this ephemeral home in paradise.

"Aye, *amigo!* Let's go surfing man!"

I walked the 20-meter pilgrimage to the beach, smoked some of Gonzalo's *hierba,* and paddled out for a morning with the Pacific waves.

"Hmm... I really want a coco," I thought aloud, catching my breath.

High tide's current had carried me nearly a kilometer southward toward a sheer mountainous point cascading into the ocean from the green inland hills. Gonzalo had returned to his beachside tent after a swell drove him in to the soft sand.

I couldn't shake this incessant urge to walk a few more kilometers for a coconut in the nearby pueblo. To my surprise, I happened to have exact change in the wax-caked pocket of my board shorts.

Gonzalo shouted broken English as the soles of my feet sizzled on crystalline salt. Eventually, his words and gesticulations became clear.

"Hey, let's go get some cocos!" he exclaimed with enthusiasm. "I'm craving one today, man!" He took a drag from his handmade pipe and tossed it to me.

"How interesting," I said, rather surprised at the timing of our mutual coconut cravings. "Me too."

"Vamanos!" he exclaimed through a waft of smoke.

Skin glowed with the warmth of the sun as we walked north along the beach. I admired the rippling surface of wet sand, the ebb and flow of burbling salt water, the microcosm of creatures, minerals, and fossils all interwoven and tossed freely about the sea. How could a vast landscape become so flooded with salt water that the many kilometers of ocean within my field of view—all the way to the gentle curve of Earth's planetary horizon—comprise no more than a dewdrop of the ocean's full immensity?

"I'm one drop of a grand sea," I introspected.

"Hey, this might sound kinda *loco*..." Gonzalo's gaze was long. Though his thick Andean accent often made his words sound like songs, many of his sentences did, indeed, sound moderately crazy. I began to imagine what he might say after such a preface, noting that his familiar playful tone had shifted into a sort of calm reverence.

"*Digame*," I said, intrigued.

He looked me straight in the eyes, without his usual chuckle. "Remember the *ayahuascero* I told you about?"

"The what?"

"The shaman," he clarified, "the wise man who knows the spirit of Ayahuasca." I nodded through a light haze of skepticism, noticing a rising feeling in my gut. Gonzalo continued, "He is there, *alla,* in the sand. Look! The way he sits, I know it."

I'd truly never considered the fact that shamans, too, go to the beach.

"Come with me," Gonzalo motioned toward the sand dunes, "I'll introduce you, you should meet him. *Despues, cocos.*"

As we approached, I noticed an easeful austerity in the man's posture. Two colorful women sat to his left. The women wore long dark hair and vibrant patterned dresses. Warm laughter erupted from the group, and the great oceanic ease coursing through my body expanded further.

The women recognized Gonzalo from a distance, warmly welcoming us in a dialect which, at the time, I had not the ears to hear. I felt gentleness and sincerity in the tone of their introductions.

The shaman focused his brilliant azure eyes into mine, extending his hand, perhaps reading the fleeting thoughts written on the inner surface of my skull. His spoken English was immaculate.

"Where do you live?" he asked, a jubilance rising from his voice.

"Well," I said, unsure of how to answer the question. "I'm from Florida, in the United States. But for now I am housesitting a few kilometers south of here." I could almost hear the synapses firing within his mind.

"Oh, Florida? Our daughter is looking into a university there. She would like to study in the United States. We were just speaking about it, actually."

The younger of the two women had focused her attention on her father's words. "Yes, just twenty minutes ago we joked, 'it would be so helpful to run into someone who knows about Florida.' How funny!"

She spoke in a clear tone, a sort of knowing in her voice. After a brief introduction, her father asked the name of the school she was interested in. "It's a small private school where I can study and learn techniques of art. It is called—"

A warm chill enveloped my body as she spoke the name of the university I had attended years prior. The family fumbled to remember the English name of the specific degree program she was interested in, though the sound of their voices was drowned in the immediate rise of my pounding heart. In that moment I was truly perplexed by what I was hearing, like witnessing a strange dream.

"I went to that university," I stumbled, pinching my own arm for good measure. "I studied—" the words left my mouth at the same moment they came to the name of her intended degree program.

We spoke the same words, in unison.

Did I really walk down this Ecuadorian coast on the whim of a coconut craving to meet a shaman whose daughter was interested in the very same art school—the very same degree program—that I attended years prior?

We've all perhaps touched upon the mysterious powers at work behind the curtains of life's grand theatre. Though, at the time, this was the clearest exposition of such underpinnings I had experienced—the coconut cravings, the exact change in my pocket, Gonzalo's presence, the happenstance of the shamans and their daughter visiting this particular beach rather than the quiet beach near their home, their conversation about the university twenty minutes prior to our introduction... This was all a bit too bizarre to be ignored.

What I didn't realize at the time: this event had little to do with my *alma mater*. This was a preliminary movement of a living spirit who had invited and enacted our introduction. She is often called Grandmother Ayahuasca.

Without this meeting, without my initial turbulent experience in Ecuador three years prior, without a broken-down van which prompted my stay at the ranch in California, without a fleeting conversation about international travels—without all of this, how would I have ended up in a chair in the pitch black of night, laughing along with a shaman as his shaking rattle facilitated a reconfiguration of consciousness in the quaking body I once believed to be my own?

An Indigenous Perspective

It is beyond the scope of this writing to adequately explain the effects of Ayahuasca, the history of its use as a ceremonial medicine, and the many stories of its existence held by indigenous practitioners. Much literature exists to describe the very many approaches to such an ineffable tradition. I will, however, give a synopsis of the perspective I received during months of preparation prior to participation in sacred ceremony with Ayahuasca.

In the vast tropical rainforest misnomered "the Amazon"—referred to here as *El Oriente*—about 80,000+ species of plants have been catalogued by modern science at the time of this writing. Many indigenous peoples of this rich land understand that every one of these plants—and perhaps everything—consists of at least a physical form (body), present awareness (mind), and a living energy (spirit), all of which manifest with a myriad of unique qualities, facets, and frequencies. The principles underlying this relationship between body, mind, and spirit are expressed quite elegantly in the imagery of the Incan Cross, a powerful symbol about which many books have been written.

When ingesting a plant in ceremonial honor and gratitude, it is said that one may merge the spirit of that plant with one's own spirit—an energetic connection occurs. The Anglo-Saxon mind often expresses an aspect of this relationship by denoting a plant's physiological and psychological affects, and within these classifications a great many plants do indeed illicit measurable psychoactive effects when ingested. It is also understood that certain plant medicines interact with and influence the expression of genes within the primary codex of physical life-forms: DNA. Ayahuasca is one of them.

Indigenous cultures of El Oriente take this one step further with the recognition of an energetic essence which animates all life—it is the beating heart of each living being, it is the sprout that cracks the seed and lifts its leaves intelligently and intentionally toward the sunlight—it is that which is, prior to the ephemeral why and how.

This vital life-energy is what many in Western culture might refer to as *spirit, soul,* or *life-force.* Polynesian cultures call it *ki* or *mana,* in India it is known as *prana,* in China it is named *chi* or *qi,* and in the indigenous tribes of the land commonly known as Ecuador, it is called *ki* or *nuna.* When this vital energy is consciously held in one's awareness and felt presently, it may be harmonized with the energy of potentially any living being. This happens to some degree when one feels love deeply, while savoring a delicious meal, or while admiring the beauty of an animal or landscape.

The essential energy and nature of plants has often been misunderstood in Western culture; the bulk of modern scientific interpretations of these plants indeed falls short in accuracy and entirety. For example, the spirit which incarnates in the form of the Tobacco plant is considered "the mother of all plant medicines" by shamans of El Oriente. Indeed, first nations all over the world have held a very similar reverence toward Tobacco for millennia. This sacred plant medicine is often misunderstood and misused in the Western world, thus deeper understanding is limited by the ways in which Tobacco and other plant medicines have been distorted and harmfully ingested.

It is said that Mother Tobacco coordinates and/or nurtures the many great plant medicines which co-exist within the rainforest. Within this perspective, Ayahuasca is said to have been born of the spirit of Tobacco many ages ago, and is respected and cared for as a grandmotherly spirit. Furthermore, this loosely generational lineage is extended to one of the many grandchildren—Psilocybin—the spirits of which are known as Children of the Light.

The living energies which inhabit these medicines are understood to be not only conscious, but also deeply involved in fostering the wellbeing and expansion of life, including the life which incarnates in the form of the human. Shamans of the past cultivated great relationships with these energies, and began to interpret and share teachings based on experiences and instructions received directly from communication with, and ingestion of, the essence of the plants. One such instruction came from a plant little-known today.

Prior to the birth of Jesus, shamans living as an integral aspect of the great rainforest communed with the spirit of this plant in ceremony. During this ceremony—so the story is told—the shamans received instructions which guided them to two specific plants of the rainforest, which were found growing in two distinct climactic zones amidst great varieties of plants hardly distinguishable from one-another through the perceptive senses and faculties available to the human being.

After being guided to these plants through the sea of green, the shamans were instructed to mix them—the root-vine of one, the leaves of the other—in a specific ratio, and set them to decoct over a flame at certain temperature-points for specific intervals of time. When all of these instructions were followed accurately and the mixture was allowed to cool, the shamans found that ingesting a small amount of the resulting brew brought them into direct contact with a being who, over two thousand years later, continues to be honored and revered in the light of sacredness.

Indeed, they were the first humans with the receptive capacity to both understand and tediously execute the steps necessary to open a grand gateway to the wise council of Grandmother Ayahuasca. Immense gratitude is the heritage of these willing souls. Thank you.

To present, innumerable traditions have developed around ceremonial communion with Ayahuasca, many of which have their roots in ancient shamanic teachings and centuries—if not millennia—of intentional exploration and cultivation.

In one such tradition, ceremony begins many weeks or months before stepping into the Alichina Wasi. A very restrictive diet is observed, consisting of light fruit, vegetable soup, and occasionally, fish. Dairy is strictly avoided, as are spices and extremes of flavor and quantity. Eating patterns and meditative practices are regulated and strictly heeded during this period of preparation.

For the week prior to ceremony, eating is weaned to 1-2 meals per day with intermittent fasting. 24 hours prior to ceremony, amidst preparatory shamanic cleansing and purification practices, no solid food is eaten—only juices and water are consumed, of which the final sip is ingested no less than 4 hours prior to ceremony.

AN INDIGENOUS PERSPECTIVE

By this process, the body is systematically cleansed of a great many inhibitive toxins and dense foods which often cause strong reactions with these ceremonial plant medicines.

With the mind centered and still, with the body cleansed, cultivated, and rooted in the present, the living energy of the spirit may be free to integrate with the living essence of the medicine.

Journal entry written prior to my first ceremony with Ayahuasca:

"Tonight, I'll experience the wonder of Ayahuasca. No control, no inhibition, simple awareness. Life, as it is. One moment human; the next, who knows. One cannot know, but simply be, as we are the unfolding cosmos and life, of itself.
I will gladly release to the wind all illusion."

The Approach

I floated through damp evening air, weaving a narrow path through lush tangles of cloud-forest vines. *Matapalo* branches and neatly-woven spiderwebs reached and clung to skin, illuminated by a distant, glowing moon. With each careful step, words seemed to sing from afar, "when you've accepted that you are lost, the Alichina Wasi will find you."

I held my inhale, listening for so much as a faint murmur, wondering at the welling uncertainty in my heart. To return? Nature's deep shadows had already reclaimed my path through the foliage. I paused, and by the time the trailing mosquitos caught up with me, I began to consider the reality that I was slowly being swallowed by the immensity of the jungle.

Only then did I notice the faint glow of a candle's flame emanating between the buds of a jasmine vine.

I stepped out of my muddy shoes, feeling the cool stroke of hand-formed clay painting the soles of my feet. Smoke rose from burning *palo santo,* dowsing a soggy palm-thatched roof. The shaman's eye flashed with the reflection of a lone candle as he lit a thick roll of tobacco leaves. I passed through the wafting space and found a chair, relaxing gently into the unknown. The shaman's dried leaf rattle began to shake gently and he cleared his throat to speak.

COSMIC JOURNEYS OF THE ALICHINA WASI

"*Alichina Wasi* can be translated 'house of healing', or 'space of transcendence,'" he began. "Elders traveled here many years ago to construct this ceremonial space by hand. It is built to host us, our spiritual energies, the many spirits of the forest and cosmos, and the sacred plant spirit, Grandmother Ayahuasca. Alichina Wasi may represent the body in which the spirit lives, and through which it may experience *cosmos* in physical manifestation.

"People of the great rainforest have ingested plant medicines for millennia in a humble quest to approach and communicate with the living spirit of these sacred plants. We do this to witness wisdom and grace with these ancient spirits, to nurture the life we embody. Tonight, you may embark on your own sacred journey."

The shaman sipped a liquid and spewed forth a powerful mist, enveloping the Alichina Wasi in a soothing fragrance. He marked the four cardinal directions and began a series of invocations to thank and invite the spirits which dwell in the volcanic peaks of Imbabura and Cotacachi, and to call upon the spirits of the forest, the jaguar, condor, serpent, the elements of nature and ancestral spirits. A living silence filled the room between the shaman's calls, jarred only by the pounding in my chest.

The shamaness lifted a bowl above her head, calling out to the spirit of Grandmother Ayahuasca in her native tongue. A simple altar of crystals, tinctures and tobacco leaves lay beneath her, surrounding a small cushion on which the bowl was placed. With a smile so warm it could ease the faintest heart, she spoke, "Trust, surrender, and gratitude are our guides."

I was invited to the altar, standing before the shamans to receive this ancient medicine. Half of a large seed shell had been dried and hollowed to serve as the drinking vessel of Ayahuasca. The shell was placed gently in the palms of my hands, which then ceased their nervous quaking. A prayer was spoken in native tongue. My empty stomach spoke and twisted as I drew the shell to my lips. Hands rose in gratitude as I tilted my head to receive the ancient medicine.

The lone candle breathed its last breath, silently vanquishing its soothing light into the great expanse of night.

JOURNEYS

JOURNEY ONE
The Mind

A tropical chorus of nocturnal voices filled a boundless black space. So rich was the deep darkness of night that time itself seemed unmoving. The body would require about 45 minutes to begin resonating with this ancient medicine.

The first taste of Ayahuasca immediately drew every iota of my being into present awareness. Immersed in the earthy musk of the Alichina Wasi and the etherial smoke of *palo santo,* the chalky brew of her ground roots and leaves enveloped every sense as it inhabited the body, permeating every possible receptor on its journey through the stomach.

I became aware of a vast silence which belayed both the songs of the jungle and the pulse of my quaking heart; both the internal and the external seemed to intertwine as aspects of one whole space. In the depth of the night, I could not perceive any boundary between "me" and this vast, all-encompassing silence.

The presence of Ayahuasca first became apparent when the heartbeat began to intensify, seemingly without impetus. Concurrently, a great upwelling of breath gave way to flashes of amber light across the screen of my closed eyes, followed by faint bursts of colors I had not seen before. These energetic movements welled up and out from within.

This rising energy continued with visions of morphing cords which seemed to be faintly luminescent, perhaps energetic. Some began to take shape as they radiated from an indistinct center, morphing into various elements of modern technology—vacuums, phone charging cords, wiggling wires.

I had a difficult time detaching from the mind's endless stream of thoughts. It kept pulling me back...

The mind whirled into thoughts of uncertainty and unrest just as it began to wander. I felt a tension between what seemed to be one aspect of my being and another, as awareness was pulled back and forth between seemingly distinct states of resistance and nonresistance.

I was brought to specific moments from childhood—extraneous memories which remerged from a catalogue buried somewhere deep within the mind's archives. One such memory drew me into a vision of a gathering at a house I visited on only one occasion, at age four or five:

I found myself standing eye-to-eye with a little girl who was rather eager to befriend me. I sensed a certain expectation—perhaps desperation—in her approach, and in reaction I opted to avoid her company.

I was there in the room, seeing through the eyes of my child-self, aware of the situation unfolding presently. I acknowledged the condition of the lighting—above, the warm hues of a tungsten bulb bled with the inflorescence of a flitting television screen. I stood leaning against the

THE MIND

cushion of a musty couch, pretending to watch the screen while I turned a cold shoulder to the eager child next to me. She soon left the room pouting, seeking solace in her mother.

Why was I shown this far-removed memory while battling between a stream of eager curiosity and the vibratory presence of Ayahuasca?

Rather than seeking, be. Rather than resisting the mind (control), let it wander. Shed the layers.

Upon returning to my room for the night, I stood in the bathroom doorway and saw my reflection dimly illuminated from behind, silhouetted mostly. The boundaries of my body were loose, undulating gently. I appeared with a subtle eminence, a faint purple-blue glow quietly radiating from beneath the surface. I did not approach the mirror—I could not see my eyes.

JOURNEY TWO
Portals of Form

The unfolding reality of All stands in beautiful cosmic array.

I fought with swaths of mosquitos and various mental fears as a welling recognition of Ayahuasca's presence began to arise.

I experienced a sort of pulling, though this pull did not interact with the body; it was in no way physical. This may be compared to a sort of magnetic attraction which seemed to draw the attention of consciousness nearer—nearer to what, I hadn't the faintest clue. My awareness was as a raft carried by an ocean current, drifting away from the sensory realm perceived through the human body, without any effort of its own. The eyes blinked in slow-motion and the physical world itself seemed to entirely disappear and reappear in the flash of an instant.

This was accompanied by a feeling so clear that I turned to the shaman and said, "Please look after my body. I'll be back." I was hesitant, with concern for the body continuing its vital processes.

"*Adonde vas?*" he asked.

"I'm not sure, but I'm going."

The shaman chuckled quietly and heartily. "Go. Your body is safe."

Awake, aware and alert, I closed my eyes and relaxed, noting that my breath was gently rising. My body began to feel quite expansive and weightless as I resigned all lingering resistance to Ayahuasca's curious effects. I recalled, *"Rather than seeking, be."*

Sensory input faded away gently, the nighttime rhapsody of toads and cicadas yielding to an awareness which, unexpectedly, felt rather familiar.

Behind closed eyelids, I began to see. Awareness drifted from the physical body seated next to the shaman. I no longer heard the shrill hum of mosquitoes drawing blood from my neck and face. I no longer felt the damp weight of humid clothes on my skin. I no longer held awareness of the heartbeat or breath. I quietly became aware of myself in another space, in another form.

I found myself perched upon the crown of Earth like an enormous toad poised atop a small stone, peering out at the surrounding cosmos. As I rose into this space, an overwhelming recognition inundated my awareness.

Something as obvious as the sand-ness of sand began to reoccur to me. "Oh, *of course!*" I exclaimed, non-verbally. "I was so caught up being that guy called Zeff! What a joke, that little human! How ridiculously attached I was! How silly!"

I remembered "who" I am: exploring the existence for millions of years, I've been around many moons. A traveler, indeed.

PORTALS OF FORM

From this vantage, it was immediately evident that for the brief flash of 24 revolutions around the Sun I had solely identified with a particular human form which completely enveloped my awareness and occupied all attention; in that same instant, I was aware of a much broader framework of my existence, one which extends far beyond the particular human life currently being lived.

This welling recognition of the greater dynamics of existence felt unequivocally obvious—like waking up on a Friday morning with the recognition that I'd lived through Thursday and Wednesday prior. I saw calmly and clearly, beyond the realm of cognitive doubt, that I had become so wrapped up in my lifetime as this particular human that I'd nearly forgotten my participation within a larger context.

I've lived all over the cosmos, and the awareness of this was crystal-clear. Though I was not immediately aware of the specific *content* of memories within this particular experience, I recognized a greater *context* of the unfolding of life. Before I could make much sense of this, a rapid chain of events began to take place, seemingly without impetus.

I first realized that the colossal body I seemed to occupy—still perched upon the Earth—appeared as little more than the phantasmic shadow of a gigantic human-like figure. Briefly, I saw this scene from afar rather than from the vantage of the "body." This form had not distinct features, but seemed a loose coagulation of the deep blackish-purple haze of the cosmic depths. The boundaries of this shadow-body were vague, despite the habitual attempt to solidify or rationalize that which eludes understanding.

In this space, an unusual creature floated slowly by. This being had a tadpole-shaped body which at first resembled brilliantly finished wood, with a few loose tufts of feathers in lieu of a tail fin and one large eye on its right side. I observed that the seemingly wooden texture of the creature's skin emitted a gentle luminescence, and was composed of thin, luminous strands morphing through subtle patterns.

This peculiar being floated on and I began to follow, gently drifting through spaciousness. Before us, a warbling yoni-shaped opening emerged. This opening, alike to a gateway or portal, felt enormous relative to typical human scale. Its edges or boundaries seemed almost aqueous, and vaginal in shape. The edges moved with gooey undulations like thick sap pouring over tree bark. How this entryway emerged I know not, but visual awareness of its presence was vivid.

Within the opening, no content stood out other than a gentle gradient of warm color which occupied nearly the whole space, fading like a cloudless sunset into the greatest distance. A deep blue-black space hung beneath, defining a sharp yet indefinite horizon. Following the peculiar creature, I drifted effortlessly through the threshold of the portal into the brilliant spaciousness within and beyond.

It became clear that the phantasmic shadow-body I seemed to occupy was indeed a sort of shadow—perhaps a psychological remnant of my former bodily awareness—which wasn't real at all. This illusory body began to gently dissolve into spaciousness, setting into motion a cascade of rapid realizations.

I instantly questioned the reality of the creature floating in front of me—which in retrospect seems no more than a sort of cosmic fishing lure. It became clear that the choice of belief alone perpetuates the apparent reality of any illusion.

My "guide" disappeared with the realization that we're not separate.

This is the threshold at which words lack the subtlety of expression necessary to directly and wholly communicate what arose—much like attempting to thread the frayed end of a string through a needle's eye. As such, I will share a visualization to attempt an explanation of the emerging relationship I felt to the expansive, luminous space within the portal:

Imagine yourself floating inside a spherical marble of cosmic proportions. Within this luminous sphere, move backward until your back is pressed against the interior surface of the marble, continuing to look inward. Imagine that the body you're associated with dissolves or integrates into the interior surface of the marble while your awareness remains; rather than an entity within the marble, it's as if you're now the marble itself, looking inwardly at your own interior.

Now, because your awareness relates to the whole interior surface of the marble, you have the potential to "see" from not just one point on the interior surface of the sphere, but from all 360° of the sphere's interior surface simultaneously.

Add one more dimension: see that the surface of the marble and its inner space are not mutually exclusive—just as the water of an ocean's surface is not fundamentally distinct from the water of the depths, and the skin of the human body is not separate from the inner space of the body—they are aspects of one whole. Within this 360° all-encompassing vantage, "you" are no longer distinct from the entirety of the marble, inside and out.

In this way, "I" seemed to expand until the entire space within the portal was observed from both the perspective of the "container" in which the space existed, and the space itself, as one integral whole.

All of existence is me. All is now. All is here, just in front of me, so to speak.

"I" became the whole of this space—or perhaps "it" became "me"—all the while maintaining a very clear awareness of "my" awareness. It was as though the consciousness which seemed to operate independently as "me" integrated with the consciousness of space itself. As such, I was existence, with no distinctions otherwise.

The experience truly felt as tangible as any wakeful experience. I felt no inclination to question the reality of what was occurring, in the same way one wouldn't typically question the reality of a morning cup of coffee. I seemed to have full access to cognition or some comparable faculty, and I maintained conscious awareness of my decisions, movements, and curiosities throughout the journey. Though I was in no way certain where, how, or why any of this was occurring, nothing about the experience seemed threatening or unnatural.

Presence momentarily snapped back into the body on Earth to find that a partially blind cat was haphazardly climbing onto my lap, sinking its claws into my leg for leverage.

"Whose leg is this, *really?*" I wondered, inwardly.

I gently relocated the cat and peered into the night as the shaman shook his leaf rattle in concert with the mystical vibrations of *icaros*—songs of the spirit which themselves seemed to be singing him. He stopped briefly and we met eyes.

"Well? Is it *your* leg?"

He erupted with laughter as I returned his question with a wild face of disbelief. He simply resumed singing.

Perplexed, I closed my eyes once more and, within an instant, was right where I had been, existing as the space within the portal.

Strange, indeed.

∞◉∞

I conjured anything ... right there, in the space of no-space.

I began to realize that any physical form could potentially exist or manifest within this grand space. I seemed to be the entirety of space—the presence which fundamentally constituted its existence. I began to wonder about all of this. Perhaps prompted by the recent sight of the curious feathered creature, I resolved to conjure up a single feather.

I centered my attention upon the idea of a feather and a feather arose, seemingly from nothingness into present awareness. I have no means of understanding or explaining "how" this happened.

After approaching the feather, entering closer and closer to a microscopic level (it appeared full-

detail to my formless, size-less existence) I became the bristle of the feather. I experienced, "briefly", its existence.

Within this state of awareness, bound to no physical entity nor any particular size or scale, I could "move" and see into any level of scale, grand or tiny.

Upon drawing near to the feather, seeing the structural components of each individual feather bristle, I wriggled into the feather itself. I "became" the feather—or more accurately, I intentionally moved inside a single tendril which split from the end of a bristle of the feather, without any distinction between "it" and "me". Though the sensation of this (or lack thereof) could be considered rather underwhelming, I was nonetheless filled with a wonderful fascination at this strange assimilation.

"What else might I be able to conjure? What else might I be?" I wondered.

I dove inside the Sun—flew right up to it and dove into the center. No sensation, just observation. I floated there, inside the Sun, laughing at the trivialities of Earth-bound life. Bug bites and worry, how hilariously silly! It's all silly! Manifested ideas within the totality of all. I was lying in the Sun!

Bright, luminous energy moved with fierce rapidity, fusing inwardly from all sides into a single, undefinable point at the center of a colossal sphere. I became the center point at which this immense central fusion occurred within the Sun. Interestingly, I hardly perceived the emission of energy in an outward direction; this would have severely contradicted the intense inward vortex. Rather, the fusion of this bright energy seemed far too strong and inescapable for much of anything to simultaneously move outwardly from the center; its luminosity seemed not composed of the *emission* of light and moving photons, but instead seemed to be the *culmination* of the essence of light itself. I basked in this inexplicable energy.

I came back and watched Earth unfold from 'afar', watched Florida become a lush jungle and a bone desert, rifts across lands and morphing oceans.

This appeared as a time-lapse through vast stretches of the past and/or future—though linear classifications seemed rather arbitrary in this state. Oceans rose and fell, life came and went through brief flashes of innumerable transient epochs.

I gave my mother a big hug. I felt our one-ness. I, we, are the Mother. I felt her physical presence in that hug.
I forgave the triviality of my dad's life. We laughed! Laughed and laughed and laughed.

I stood facing the man who helped give rise to the physical incarnation I see through. A man I hadn't interacted with since shortly after birth. A man who ended his own human life years before I resigned my efforts to contact him.

To see him standing in front of me, in comedic poise, was perhaps one of the greatest wonders of this lifetime. To look into the eyes of his spirit while acknowledging that the context of existence is so incomprehensibly boundless relative to the fleeting psychological phenomena of the content of our lives... all we had was pure, genuine laughter. It was the laugh of immense healing and relief.

How silly, what a game, a play. It became clear that the world isn't necessary. If it wasn't for my mother, for her physical sake, I felt no real clear reason to remain in this body. I just kept laughing at the manifestations. I didn't have to come back.

I became more curious about all of this... so far I'd seen forms and colors, life. What creates life, I wonder? What's that like? It surely is here, everything is here (including the physical body I'd touch base with periodically). And then...

I was drawn away from the space of manifestation in which I had conjured first the feather, then the Sun, then the interaction with my father. The scene seemed to move away in space and become distant, as if I was flying backward and away, drifting out of the yoni portal through which I entered. I did not occupy a body.

The space surrounding this awareness became increasingly bright, glowing radiantly as the portal faded into the great expanse. I seemed to fly backward through a tunnel of luminescent whiteness, yet I experienced no sensation of movement. Perhaps it is most accurate to say that the space of the scene itself moved through my awareness like wind through a screen, initially giving the impression that I was moving in reverse.

The luminous tunnel opened to a massive triangle of life / light. Colossal in scale, it was as if all was simultaneously sucked into this triangle as I moved through it, backward, revealing a scene of glistening grey ethereal clouds, moody blues and golden light, bright white within the open portal of the triangle.

I observed the wall of this gateway. The closer I got, the more subtle colors and tessellating kaleidoscope of geometry; what seemed like solid matter was anything but.

The whole gateway through which I emerged stood before me. The scene appeared to float in a deep, undefined spaciousness. I saw the bright white tunnel of light glowing within the triangular gateway.

Though the structure of the gateway itself appeared metallic from afar, upon closer inspection I found it to be made up of subtly undulating patterns. It seemed to be arranged with a great depth of fineness, exhibiting incalculable patterns, shapes, and luminous colors. In retrospect, it is clear that the cosmic fishing lure I saw earlier in the journey appeared with a very similar composition. The clouds passing in front of the gateway may not have been composed of water vapor, but seemed to be reflecting or even emanating a sort of golden-grey luminosity. As a whole, the gateway exhibited a presence not unlike that of a colossal theme-park entrance.

I became aware that this gateway serves as an entrance to the realm of form-based reality—within this portal exist physical matter, bodies, waves, particles, galaxies, color, every facet and nuance of the cosmos of form. I had essentially moved from within this gateway, out of it.

This gave way to a profound shift in understanding of the context of existence. Never had I conceived of physical, form-based life being contained only within a particular sector of reality; nor would I have conceived that this sector of reality was marked by and entered into via a colossal inverted-triangle-shaped gateway. Most of all, "my" human mind hadn't yet fathomed the potential of existence beyond the bounds of physicality altogether.

In an eternal moment of stillness and observation, another undoubtably curious aspect of this became clear: I could, at will, bring my awareness into the physical body on Earth, seated next to the shaman, opening the eyes and recognizing physical reality as experienced through the sensory nodes of the human. I could then close my eyes and, within an instant, return to the vantage of the triangular gateway. I had conscious access to both spaces, but presence was perhaps only possible in one space at a time. I intentionally shifted awareness back and forth a few times, at will. In each instance, "I" seemed to flow through the great triangular gateway.

Curiosity arose and asked, "If all of form is contained within this gateway, and 'I' am outside of said gateway, then what is out here?"

I recognized that, due to the manner in which this scene arose, I had yet to see what was behind my field of view. I decided to "turn around" (though I had no association with a body) to see what could possibly exist beyond this gateway to the realm of physical reality.

A high degree of cognitive dissonance set in rather instantly. What I saw expanded in all directions, occupying the whole of space.

PORTALS OF FORM

I beheld a kaleidoscopic array of color and light, not reflecting color but embodying it in rippling 'ribbons' of colored patterns. Somewhat similar to Otavalan textiles, to a degree. I was spinning my head around physically, and dimension itself was undulating in this formless representation of changing pattern and light.

Colossal bands of luminescent colors and patterns, which seemed to contain highly energetic properties, comprised the entirety of this field. This stood before me like an infinite wall of astounding breadth and depth; the threshold of this space was undulating and morphing like the surface of an ocean.

This struck conscious awareness with such profundity that, one could say, the rational mind was completely blown. The ineffability, the innate beauty of such an unusual sight incited immense wonder.

I could no longer hold presence there. The mind, to whatever extent it was present, could not compute this immense field. Upon a momentary attempt to ascertain some level of comprehension, awareness was forced through the triangular gateway, warping through the bright whiteness from whence I came, through the yoni portal, and in an instant I felt my presence rocket back into the human body, crashing into physical reality exactly as a meteorite strikes the surface of the Earth. The eyes ripped open with a gasp and I looked out in wild wonder, not believing the sheer might behind this warping of conscious awareness, not understanding what had occurred, perplexed at my immersion in these expansive aspects of reality.

Somehow, the attempt to distill this warping space into the confines of cognition seemed to cause the instantaneous ejection of awareness from that space.

Shortly thereafter, I felt a knot twist deep within the stomach, which quickly sent the physical body staggering to the railing of the balcony to purge—this came with an entirely different quality to vomiting. As the stomach was mostly empty after many days of intermittent fasting, what occurred was a strong upwelling of energy which poured out of my being. The sensation of this was not unlike that which occurs when vehemently screaming into a pillow or expelling extremely intense emotions. This poured forth from the depths of being, flashed through awareness, and eventually culminated as waves of waning intensity and waxing relief.

True to the cosmic joke, I found myself haphazardly giggling as this intensity took place. I watched the body writhe in the discomfort and momentary anguish of dry-heaving, recognizing the various sirens and alerts sounding within the body's complex mechanisms, and laughed even more. Amidst this I understood the joyousness of this powerful release, the naturalness, the right-use-ness of this sacred moment. Gratitude rose through my being, and I soon relaxed back into the chair.

After throwing up and laughing at how seriously the body was taking this, I sat down and wondered about what manifests forms. Oh beautifulness!

I witnessed the seed of life, unfolding! A bright white-blue-purple-hued sphere, undulating and morphing in simultaneous stillness. The flower / seed of life pattern wrapped the bottom of the sphere. It had roots hanging below, reaching into the pitch-black 'space' of no-thing, pure emptiness. Somehow, this is what manifests material into the physical plane, perhaps life, in the 3rd dimension.

This sight can be described as a glowing cluster of energy suspended in open spaciousness, with a distinct horizon line below. Flares of light shot out from the surface of the cool luminous sphere; these whipping wisps and bands of energy then became physical manifestations, somehow formed from the size-less yet seemingly gigantic orb, perhaps shooting out toward the place in which they would manifest. I don't recall the content to a great extent of specificity, but these were clearly physical and celestial objects—bodies, materials, planets—being emitted and launching into the surrounding spaciousness on beams of energy alike to those witnessed within a plasma globe.

The energy for this seemed to come up through the roots hanging from the lower portion of the sphere, which 'dipped" below the horizon line into empty black spaciousness. This formless space seemed completely devoid of any content whatsoever, save for the roots of the orb. The roots appeared to drink from the emptiness, usurping whatever is necessary for the spawning of forms. I acknowledged awe, reverence, and wonder at the beauty and aliveness of this coalescing energy. Though I acquired not the faintest idea as to how, where, or why it exists, I could not avoid the overwhelming recognition of the actuality of its existence amidst the great expanse.

All the while, healing and love and food and money became a big joke. How simple, how easy! Life is here, life is all of this. No separation, actually; just illusion. Bizarre, beautiful.

Amongst these realms, Earth is one of an infinite array of worlds and possibilities. Ants rove about the surface, insignificant but aspects of the totality. I kept wondering why. Why physical bodies? Why come back? Why would I feel inclined to "save the world" if it's all one, me, Self, existence's manifestation among infinitely happening scenarios? Why?

It is clear that I can go about this goofy Earth doodleedoo sans worry and fear; life is sacred in origin and boundless in scope.

JOURNEY THREE
The Council of Duality

The heart began to thump. It wasn't nervous, not excited, not fearful; but powerful.

I was overcome by a distinctly tremendous quality of the heartbeat and breath, similar to that which I experienced during the first journey. The rising energy within the body quite rapidly and powerfully overrode any control I may have wished to exert, drawing awareness into a new space, without resistance.

Behind closed eyes, I became aware of a space which looked like a simple, well-lit courtroom with plain walls and plain wooden tables. A council meeting was soon to begin. I observed patiently, assuming myself to be a simple spectator to this peculiarly formal scene.

The meeting seemed to be coming together rather spontaneously, without prior planning or anticipation. I had the impression that clerical workers were shuffling around the room, hastily organizing as the meeting spawned into existence; though, neither humans nor any other distinct forms of beings were observed. One cannot say positively that any physical entities existed in the seemingly physical space, as the numerous energies observed seemed only as physical as, perhaps, gusts of wind.

Indeed, as the energies moved about the room, their movements created momentary trails alike to that which occurs when a person walks quickly through thick smoke. These trails carried very faint tints of soft hues.

As the meeting continued to take shape, two primary energies began to emerge—one to the left and one to the right. Though the setting was clear to the inner vision, these emerging energies were at first only vague, spherical hazes. They each emanated a force which interacted with the other in a way alike to magnetic polarity, as one seemed to mutually "counter" the other. This polarity was not necessarily felt as one would feel the force of opposing magnets, but it was the foremost quality discerned by observation without tactile sensation.

As in the previous journey, a sort of dual-presence was experienced: at will, I opened the eyes with what seemed to be full awareness of the physical "real world", noting a gentle beam of moonlight trickling through the thatched roof of the Alichina Wasi. Upon closing the eyes, awareness again returned to the council meeting setting.

The two distinct energies of the council steadily grew in presence as the breath of the physical body grew mightier. The breath seemed to draw these immense energies nearer to one-another. As the chest cavity filled to a volume not previously experienced, it became clear that these seemingly disparate realms were intimately entwined.

The tone of the council meeting had shifted from that of pending formalities to one of austerity, with undercurrents which felt like reverence. This coincided with a gathering of various energetic presences not directly associated with distinct forms or bodies, but which seemed to embody subtle opaque hues in the lower foreground of the field of vision. Some of these energies seemed earthy-red, others citrine-yellow, others were less obvious. I noted their presence only momentarily, as I was quickly inundated by a looming reality:

"I" was the presiding entity here; "my" body was the courthouse in which this great meeting was held.

I came to realize that the courtroom was a rather obvious facade or symbolic stage-set; concurrently, I was filled with an understanding that this meeting place was located within the deeply pounding heart of my physical body.
This gave way to the recognition that I would soon be in charge of conducting a meeting of the two eminent energies, which had grown into powerfully radiant swirling spheres alike to stars.

I considered the Chakra teachings I've been exposed to recently... the heart is the connection between the ethereal and the physical, between the Great Spirit and Mother Earth. It's the point at which they come together, and it is through the channel of this body that they can become one, like a straw being sipped of water.

One peculiar connotation within this journey was the sense of novelty about the meeting, and it led to the pondering of a broader scope of humankind's existence.
The dual energies seemed to stand as representations or embodiments of the dual powers often represented in many cultures; Yin and Yang, Sun and Moon. These thematic opposites, often represented as light and

dark or masculine and feminine, can be defined in most of life: magnets have two opposing poles, DNA strands form pairs, gender is often anatomically binary, each color in the human spectrum has a compliment and every "yes" has a "no".

Many of these polar relationships are very much rooted in properties of measurable physics—they're baked into the dynamics of human life. We can also observe this relationship in the physical structure of many animals, plants, and fungi: the great majority of animal bodies form symmetrically as cells divide into equal pairs, the two sides of the body growing to reflect each other relative to a center point or line. Whether fern, palm, fruit tree, hardwood, grass or other, the structure of most plant leaves is reflected symmetrically along a central vein. From the highest flying birds to the tiniest microorganisms in the depths of the sea, nearly all beings on Earth are comprised of equal yet opposite aspects which, when taken together, give rise to the dynamics of one living whole.

This is dualism: the conceptual understanding of seemingly distinct opposites which stand at equal length to a mutual, equilibrial center. And indeed, for dualism to exist conceptually, necessarily its opposite, non-dualism, must also exist by definition. A natural extension of the observation of dualism is the recognition that all opposites are inseparable aspects of one whole.

One aspect of humanity's existence is our capacity to not only perceive and define dualistic relationships, but to transcend the limitations imposed by living exclusively within the bounds of these conceptual relationships. By pondering the broader context of the realm of opposites—by viewing all opposites simultaneously as one whole—we may see a way beyond the realm of *yes* and *no, us* and *them, good* and *bad*. Both within and beyond these contextual opposites lie depths immeasurable and unspeakable. While we may glimpse this in daily life, through meditation, or in the Alichina Wasi, a sure scope of the context in which all opposites exist and which all opposites comprise still seems largely phantasmic in the minds of most humans alive today.

The two great powers met last night. I sat the Great Spirit and Mother Earth in the same "room".

A great profundity was felt in the presence of the two colossal powers which held their respective polarities to either side of me—Mother Earth to the left and Great Spirit to the right. These energies represented form and formlessness, female and male, physical and ethereal, respectively. For these two colossal aspects of reality to come together, to nearly touch, was rather marvelous—to consider their oneness was far from any consideration I alone had yet entertained.

The space stood still with a sense of calm uncertainty, like the hush which washes over spectators when an act is to be performed. This was, indeed, the state of my heart. The gathering of smaller energies seemed to simply spectate—I, too, was curious to witness this unfolding.

Could it be that "I" was summoning this great feat in the universe? What were we here for?

I began to wonder at humankind's role in the fusion of these dynamic aspects of reality. To what extent is this polarization a mere illusion of perception? Is there a present reality to this relationship, or is it merely based on cognitive classifications? Can these opposites be reconciled, forming what would appear to be a greater, transcendent whole?

Was this simply occurring within my independent consciousness? Is "my" consciousness truly separate from the consciousness living in all of life's forms? Was this meeting representative of the whole of living reality, or of just "me"? Are they one and the same? What could come of this meeting?

Though I began to accept my role as the conductor of this meeting, I wasn't entirely sure how to go about it, nor did I understand the scope or purpose of the meeting. Rather, I recognized the opportunity to listen, to hear what the great half-wholes of reality may wish to express. Surely, upon hearing their expressions I could potentially conduct this meeting with intention.

I asked them each to state their case, as this council meeting was still rather formal at this point. I asked Mother Earth to come forward, to speak.

At once, upon giving the floor to Mother Earth, rain began to pour.

In physical reality, above the roof of the Alichina Wasi, at the very instant I "gave the floor" to the energetic presence understood to be Mother Earth within the journey, clouds opened and an unprecedented deluge of rain began. Rain poured down with such immediate power that I was roused from the vision and quickly opened my physical eyes, stunned at the synchronicity of these events. Wind whistled through the splayed bamboo walls and heavy raindrops plopped through the thatched

roof. Crickets shrilled, toads wropped, nightbirds called with vigor—every voice of the jungle awoke, singing in a cacophony which echoed the booming voice of thunder rolling overhead. This occurrence was confirmed with certainty the following morning.
Mother Nature, Patchamama, truly spoke.

I asked the Great Spirit to speak. The Spirit, despite all the magnificence it could display, expressed noble silence amidst this powerful council.

In physical reality, all sounds ceased as quickly as nature's intensity had come moments prior—each animal, insect and raindrop quelled its expression in concert. A powerful silence issued forth, which was rich with aliveness yet entirely devoid of content—this perplexing shift was also confirmed the following morning by fellow journeyers.
I was becoming aware of a greater context in which this unfolding meeting had its existence, and its relationship with physical reality. I wondered at the implication of this meeting unfolding deep within the heart of the body.
Everything Mother Earth is, Great Spirit is not, and vise-versa. Their dualistic relationship was clearly displayed, and therein, the limitations of the exclusivity of their polarity became obvious. With this recognition, some aspect of their relationship seemed to be moving toward reconciliation.

Spirit knows not physical connection. Earth knows not space. They must meet. They must experience the other side...

I began to directly interact with Mother Earth. Now viewing planet Earth from perhaps the moon's vantage, I watched an opening form in her subtly glowing atmospheric aura.

Great Mother Earth is dense. She holds everything in. I gave her space to release the excess, the CO_2 in the upper atmosphere; the built-up tension of Earth rose up and out into space. Release.

I witnessed Mother Earth expel a dense mass of many toxins in a colossal sigh of release. I saw an opening briefly form in the atmosphere through which the accumulation of pressure, chaotic energies and heavy contamination were released. This gave way to a momentary spacious emptiness, a noble silence, within the easeful nature of her form. A feeling of deep relief and lightness emanated through the entirety of awareness.

The Great Spirit knows nothing but spacious weightlessness. I wrapped my arms around the Spirit, giving a glimpse into physical connection; simultaneous individuality and connection.

Arms as colossal as the sphere in which infinity exists stretched to envelop the formlessness of Spirit in a hug unlike any other. This hug seemed to introduce an aspect of being to non-being—the unifying connection of an embrace between two seemingly distinct bodies or forms. The essence of One was held in the love of Two.

It became clear that Great Spirit and Mother Earth were beginning the process of coalescence, and that humanity is the manifested connector.

Here's where a transcendence of the polar, dualistic relationship was glimpsed. As two seemingly disparate aspects of a truly unitary whole, these powers are only separate within the context of perception, experience or identification, whether within the individual human or in life collectively. As soon as form and formlessness are viewed from a holistic standpoint, it's rather evident that these powers cannot fundamentally exist separately, though a conceptual line may be drawn to divide them.

It seemed that both energies shared a compulsion to come together, to unite. Perhaps the limitations of separation are enough to prompt a movement toward holism, which may give way to a presence far greater than the sum of its parts.

It was clear that not just Earth and Spirit were meeting, but the Form and the Formless. I began to channel the non-physical down through the body, linking it with the physical and bringing it into density. For the physical to become non-physical, it had to rise outside of the body. I moved my hands in large circles to channel these colossal energies, blending them gently.

This was the first time I intentionally conducted energy as one would during a practice like QiGong or Reiki. The motions were inseparably syncopated with the breath; with arms raised above the head, I inhaled the energy of formlessness through the crown of the head as the hands moved down the sides of the body past the hips, palms facing inward. I then exhaled the energy of physicality as the hands extended forward from the root, circling out and upward until the arms were again extended above the head. This was repeated countlessly, the breath expanding further with each cycle.

It became obvious that the true blending of the great perceived forces would mean a colossal rearrangement of all of life. No "existence" as such. No Earth, no Spirit, but a paradoxical fusion and dissolution of all, into one.

Now, All stood at the threshold of absolute unification—the door was wide open, so to speak. The impending marriage of these two powers might necessarily mean the sacrifice of both of them, which may in turn give rise to a new creation—not unlike the metamorphosis of a caterpillar, which practically dissolves within the chrysalis so as to remerge a grand butterfly.

With the arms and breath still powerfully circulating and blending the energies of form and formlessness through the human vessel, the once-polar energies of Mother Earth and Great Spirit radiated expansively and powerfully, as two stars coalescing and merging toward their mutual center.

Amidst this highly energized moment I became awash with uncertainty and hesitation rooted in fear. Having only a provisional understanding of the whole context of what was occurring, I questioned deeply the implications of this union. While it may be that the whole unfolding of this meeting pertained to nothing outside of "my" individual psyche, the tone communicated throughout the vision reached far beyond any conceptualization of "me" as distinct from the whole of reality.

"I" saw this beginning to happen, through "me."

If this was, indeed, a cosmic event, then what authority might "I" have to enact such a profound union? Why would it occur in this individual, and what about the rest of humanity? Would all of this—the great rainforest, the unexplored oceans, the great sun and every home under it—all melt away through some sort of metamorphosis, as does the caterpillar? Surely the Great Whole of All must be extraordinary, but could I really make this decision on behalf of potentially all forms of life? Am I distinct from that Life?

These contradictory thoughts, and a rising fear born of the fracture of an illusory individual self, took hold of presence. What I can recall from within the intensity of swirling, coalescing energy is a self-induced hesitation, a sort of choking of the engine, which caused the extraordinary process to gradually slow down. What felt like a luminous universal fusion began to dissipate like a hurricane without access to warm water. The breath was quite vexed as I recognized just how close the two energies came to union. Whether this was solely a personal experience or whether the context was, indeed, indicative of the whole of life, uncertainty and fear of the unknown overrode this rising movement.

Ego stepped in and clouded the vision. It was clear, through the recognition of the "I", that "I" was not ready to enact this process, to completion.

However, it has begun.

I was impaired by the mind and its rattling. I began attempting to direct, rather than listening. When I finally did purge, it was quite intense. I threw up what little I had, but the body continued heaving; what left was not physical at that point. I had an inkling that my brain attachment was spewing forth, though there's work left to be done. Poco a poco... Shed the layers until only the One is left.

If intended for entertainment or recreation, the unfolding of this journey could certainly be deemed anticlimactic. Rather, one is invited to ponder the potentiality and implications of this union, if the idea of this union isn't, itself, an illusion.

What might this mean for you, for me, for us, for the "I" which belies I-dentity? Why might you be reading this? And truly, who is writing this? Who sees through the eyes, reads, interprets, breathes, experiences the life being lived? Is that self partial, or is it integral, one with all that is?

How might one amalgamate the dualistic polarities of reality through one's own being? Is it even necessary or possible if all is truly One? If so, may this union be embodied without the safe haven of the Alichina Wasi, without the guidance of shamans, without Grandmother Ayahuasca's immense presence? Does anything truly change or become integrated, or do only the erroneous conceptions of dualistic relationships fall away to reveal an ever-integral whole? How might these questions be explored and integrated into living reality?

To quote the shaman: "A question is a quest-I'm-on."

Where to, dear One?

JOURNEY FOUR
By the Wings of Humanity

I was smeared across the universe like a fresh coat of marmalade.

I quickly found myself on the "other side"; the physical eyes were closed as conscious awareness was alive and active. I occupied what seemed to be a representation of the same body I physically inhabit, as nothing felt abnormal or foreign. I stood in a natural landscape, very clearly on Earth. It was a hilly, grassy place, with scattered dwarfen trees. Nothing seemed unusual about the setting to the focused observation.

Lying face-down near the apex of a small grassy hill was a human body. This body was idle just long enough to rouse my curiosity, and with this open curiosity I approached. In this awareness no verbal communication occurred, but as I stood looking down at the body I understood that this being's physical form was a representation or embodiment of humanity as one whole, integral being.

From the back of the idle body sprouted a very large pair of wings. They appeared somewhat feathered, though there was an unusual quality to them. The feathers were grayish, and had a texture alike to the surface of a beetle's exoskeleton. The body began to rise off of the ground but was not necessarily lifted by the wings—this luminous being seemed rather to awaken and gently float from the grassy knoll, rising into the spaciousness above.

It was understood that I was to follow. Without an attempt to question, I took flight and rose off of the ground, feeling a slight anxiousness at the distance which had grown between myself and this apparent embodiment of humanity. I caught up as we ascended out of Earth's atmosphere. There was no physical sensation of flight, no lack of air or need to breathe, no sense of exertion. We simply went, gaining a spectacular view of the curvaceous Earth and her natural majesty.

We flew into open space. The great expanse was entirely devoid of sensation after my initial amazement. We flew through the solar system, away from the sun, for what seemed to be a truly astronomical length of time.

We passed close by Jupiter, pausing our flight briefly. This was extraordinary to witness. I felt the massiveness of its occupancy of space, the energy of this presence which to some degree may be expressed by its gravity. It was so vivid, clear, perhaps even somewhat luminous of itself.

After this brief visage, I was aware of myself growing disinterested, as great epochs of time seemed to elapse as we flew through vast emptiness. There seemed to be no end. Concerned that I may have trailed off, I shifted my awareness back to the physical body in the Alichina Wasi—Grandmother's chronology is rather loosely strung.

A rippling umbilical cord of light, strung from the crown of my head, grew with each breath, reaching into deep cosmos.

As I sat in the dark of night in the Alichina Wasi, my breath became very powerful in relation to the physical body. Each inhale seemed to send extraordinary amounts of energy into every cell of the body. Each exhale saw denser energy being drawn out from the body. The breath continued to deepen significantly, becoming quite audible and vigorous; I was becoming familiar with the power of the breath in the midst of this potent medicine. Though, this time, the energy of the breath seemed to reach toward the crown of the head.

The body experienced an exceptionally clear channel or vein of energy rising up along the spine, through the neck and head, and crowning at the top of the skull. As this energetic rising intensified and deepened, I at first felt as though there was no place else for the energy to go; it slammed into the top of the skull and seemed to coalesce there with each cycle of breath, nearly painfully.

Little by little, as this gathering of bright, powerful energy intensified, it began to push its way out of the crown of the head—at first in seemingly microscopic increments—all the while moving in direct accordance with the breath. As this continued to intensify, an energetic protrusion rising from the top of the skull became more defined, beginning to form a snake-like cord of bright energy—in that moment, the mind defined it as a luminous noodle. This continued for close to an hour, by human measure. I was fully present in the process, expanding the lungs to unbelievable capacity, guiding the energy upward with the hands. The cord of light grew immeasurably, first reaching through the palm-thatched roof of the Alichina Wasi into the open air above, then out through Earth's atmosphere.

The umbilical cord also became the string in string theory. I saw the fractal of the huge and the tiny, springing forth from one-another.

This wiggly cord of luminous energy grew to astronomical length—quite literally—reaching so far into the cosmos that I eventually resigned all attempts to understand its purpose or intended direction. This was intimately synchronized with the welling sensations within the body, and coincided with the rising eminence I felt within. I had no clue if this cord of light reached for a particular place, or if it was connecting to something in particular—I made no attempt to control it. I could not consciously resolve an understanding of this cord of light, if such a resolution was to be reached consciously.

Seemingly without impetus, awareness was called back to the interminable interplanetary flight following the winged embodiment of humanity—perhaps this is where the cord of light was reaching.

We were now closing in on what was understood to be Pluto's atmosphere; a relatively small, blue-hued planetary body. As we descended toward the planet, the blue hue gave way to a less saturated shade of cool grey. As the surface of the planet was coming into clearer view, I noticed a long rectangular area with many organized lines and shapes.

As we approached, this rectangular development looked to be an extremely large computer chip or circuit board with path-lines running between various blocks and nodes, all connected to what appeared to be a central hub powering the complex.

Closer yet, I began to see that this "computer chip" was comprised of buildings, walkways and/or roads—the various "nodes" were structural and quite obviously intentional in design. There wasn't much color distinction to be noted. I felt perplexed by this structural organization—despite some skepticism, it was again understood that we were descending onto Pluto.

We continued our approach, now flying directly toward the complex from above. We descended toward the largest structure, indeed a core of the elaborate circuitry.

When we were within perhaps a few hundred feet of the surface of the pale blue-hued planet, I saw that the main core was an irregularly shaped, tent-like structure, with a white roof draping between structural columns—much like a massive, sprawling circus tent. As we landed, I recall passing straight through the roof of the tent structure near the entrance—we did not move through a doorway.

At this point, I was no longer aware of the winged body which had led me to this place. I'm not sure where this being may have gone, or if it was present as the journey continued. I'm certainly grateful for the graciously patient, non-verbal guidance across what was understood to be our local solar system.

I was now alone—or so I thought—inside the vastly spacious tent, which had nearly no end in sight. All was awash with muted warm-grey tones. Within the tent stood dozens of rows of long, straight tables extending in seemingly endless lines away from where I stood. These were alike to long cafeteria tables, with only very narrow spaces between the backs of each row. I recognized that the space was absolutely silent—or perhaps I had no ears with which to hear, or no air upon which sound may travel.

Seated along both sides of every table, practically elbow to elbow, were human beings; thousands of humans, seated silently as far as eyes could see within this giant structure. They sat completely motionless in plain, colorless clothing, each wearing a strange sort of headgear.

I understood that I wasn't to disturb anything in this space. *"Am I even supposed to be in here?"* I wondered. Nobody was present to monitor the motionless place. I moved freely, and decided to approach one of the tables to inspect further.

I walked up one row and stood behind a man, noting that all of the headsets looked identical, with wires and cables running to/from them. I don't recall what these were attached to. Each body sat facing a sort of small cubical, with dividers placed on the blank tables slightly separating each person. No sounds, no expressive content, no movement whatsoever. Each headgear appeared like a sort of virtual-reality device; this was the initial understanding while investigating this unusual place.

Still standing behind the man, I wanted to know what he was experiencing within the headgear. I moved in very closely, situating myself just behind and slightly below his right ear, where the edge of the headset rested against his short dark hair. I did not disturb the man, but instead gently squeezed my presence up under the edge of the headset and into it, into his mind, into his consciousness, to experience what he was experiencing. This seemed like an obvious approach in the moment, though I look back and wonder at the fluidity of this action.

Upon entering this man's experience, I found myself in a lush, green landscape, with a brilliant blue sky sprinkled with cumulus clouds and bright green treetops sprawling into the distance. A grassy, neatly landscaped space occupied most of my view. A lightly-traveled path winded along in the foreground toward the edge of the grassy space, near a line of understory trees which was closer yet. My view of this place was from an elevated position. I saw humans walking casually along the path down below as a gentle breeze blew. A calm, beautiful land; perhaps a spacious public park.

Noting the vibrance of this scene—especially in relation to the drab grayness of the Plutonic tent structure—I felt inclined to explore. *"What is this place? Where am I?"* I wondered. Indeed, it seemed to feel exactly as Earth feels. I wanted to investigate, so I attempted to move. However, this attempt was futile.

I could not move and did not immediately understand why; I only gently swayed. Slowly, it became clear that I was not inhabiting a human body, nor any kind of body remotely close to that which I had perhaps anticipated—I had neither legs nor the ability to move about this brilliant landscape of my own accord. The body seemed somehow rooted in place.

As I looked upon myself, I realized that I occupied the body of a tall tree overlooking the peaceful landscape. I acknowledged my branches, quivering thin leaves, and the gentle ease of swaying stillness. This rather amazed me, and to this day has given way to a great reverence for the aliveness and perceptive capacity of trees, here on Earth.

Tree-being is the same feeling as human-being, just limited mobility. Like wishing I could fly, trees want to walk.

There I was, experiencing the easeful existence of a tree within a strange virtual-reality headgear worn by an immobile man in a peculiar tent which stood as the central node of a development of structures arranged in the likeness of a giant computer chip on the surface of Pluto—all of which I arrived at through the silent guidance of an embodiment of humanity which sprouted wings and flew across the solar system within my conscious awareness during a sacred Ayahuasca ceremony.

Strange, indeed.

However, within this experience my curiosity was not satiated, and having no option of mobile exploration within this man's experience, I decided to back out of it after observing the scene.

I recoiled somehow, backing out of this existence, out of the man's conscious awareness, out of the headset, and back into the grey, motionless tent on Pluto.

I looked to the right, at a woman seated next to the man. In the same way I entered the man's experience, I seeped into the headset behind her left ear. "Is she experiencing something else?" I wondered.

Upon flowing into this woman's perception, I understood that I was viewing perhaps the same lush, green, manicured park, but this time I was very clearly operating a human body, strolling leisurely along a lightly-traveled trail with two or three other people.

I was simultaneously shocked and elated at this opportunity to move freely within the mysteriously ordinary space, and at the ability to interact with what appeared to be other humans. I seemed to fully occupy this woman's conscious experience.

My first exclamation toward the people with whom I found myself walking was that of amazement, and specifically, amazement at the fact that we were wandering around in such an immersive, extraordinarily detailed "simulation of Earth." I expressed these wild recognitions, and the fact of actually being on Pluto, seeking input and possibly explanation from these people.

Toward my immediate exuberance they seemed astounded, entirely dense, and put-off; I can't quote their words exactly, but they essentially looked at me as though I was a lunatic, perhaps even laughing at my assertions which jarred their peaceful stroll.

Though I recognized that this was perhaps not a "real" place—that it was somehow linked to the headgear worn by the people in the tent—not one person within the experience had any concept of being in a simulated experience; everyone was living, existing, reacting, and emoting as though this was an entirely genuine world, a completely real experience. Upon my insistence, the group disbanded, more or less telling me to get my head checked. I was flabbergasted, and attempted to find others within this experience who might listen.

The experience I had here was rich. I did a great deal of walking, searching, and asking throughout the journey, which seemed to span a length of many days, though the 'sun' never set. There was no nightfall for the duration of my journey there. I navigated a town and other hilly landscapes, approaching and speaking with many people, but my assertions were poorly received. I felt momentary inklings of doubt toward my own assertions, but quickly shook these for fear of becoming stuck in unreality.

I intended to somehow demonstrate the artificiality of the world in which all of these people were immersed and by which they seemed to be so entirely hoodwinked. I speculated about some sort of exit, some way out of this experience from within, which may at least demonstrate this realm's existence within a broader context. "Perhaps I can find it," I thought.

I knew I could simply pull my conscious awareness out of this woman's headgear to find myself on Pluto, just as I had after the man-tree's experience, but all others with whom I interacted seemed entirely immersed in the experience, as they understood this to be their true conscious existence, without question.

Eventually, I found myself conversing with a few people who seemed to acknowledge the sincerity back of my tenacity. Intrigued by my insistence, they accepted the idea that I had arrived in this immersive "virtual" realm through a warping of my consciousness into a headset worn by an idle stranger on a faraway celestial body. We agreed to search together for a way out of this experience.

Through a series of logistical events, I set out with this small group of interested people across a distant landscape. It was a hilly, grassy place, with scattered dwarfen trees.

We combed the land for hours like a search party. Eventually we came to a stone pillar about one meter tall, with what appeared to be a large red button attached to the top. This was understood to be a means of exit—almost too cliché to be believable, yet there it was. All of us stood perplexed, and I most certainly became excited, as anyone would surely find this an extremely peculiar item to be situated far away from anything or anyone amidst a moorish, tree-pocked land. Perhaps the sheer peculiarity of this artifact was enough to compel their curiosity.

I pressed the button, but this did not seem to affect anything. Perhaps it required something more. I, too, began to wonder if I was searching for a lost cause.

Amidst uncertainty and lack of clarity as to how to go forward, I left this search to the others within the experience. Having gone this far, I again insisted that this was indeed a virtual experience which they could somehow exit, and that they would likely find themselves in a massive tent on Pluto upon doing so. I made them aware of my departure, of my conscious recognition of where I was going, and we bid farewell. I backed out of the woman's experience in the presence of these congenial people.

I do wonder if the woman's consciousness regained control as I backed out of her virtual awareness. This was the final means by which I hoped to demonstrate the truth of my assertions. I did not attempt to " re-enter" her experience after retreating.

I returned to the dull gray tent on Pluto where the woman's body sat undisturbed, and I walked outside. Leading from the doorway of the giant tent was a sidewalk which extended between classroom-sized buildings alternating on either side of the path. Everything about the place seemed to say, "Authorized Personnel Only". I walked as far as the first building on the left, then back alongside the tent structure. Upon the rising of fear—and uncertainty of my permission to rove about this bizarre place—in conjunction with a sense of absolute exhaustion, I opened the physical eyes on Earth.

I arose once more to the sounds of the shaman's spirit songs as my heart beat like living thunder. Had I the endurance of focus, or perhaps total fearlessness, I may have explored further in the circuit board complex, perhaps uncovering more understanding about the space, about the nature of the experience of the thousands of people in the tent, about the apparent reality of the existence of this place on our solar system's demoted planet.

Perhaps the vehement assertions made within the headgear began some level of investigation from within.

Upon beginning a wobbly walk back from the Alichina Wasi, a fantastic display of tiny orange lights flashed amidst the air of dense tropical vegetation; a tribe of fireflies was passing through the jungle. I walked immersed in their light, which gave the space a glow alike to a candle's flame by which I was able to see.

Colorful winged creatures float on the wind, travel the world and suck in the sweet nectar of flowers for vitality. Fireflies show me that life is a beautiful unfolding paradise and we're here to enjoy it, perhaps learn some things, then the 'game' ends.

JOURNEY FIVE
Ego's Waiting Room

Each time I entered the Alichina Wasi for ceremony I chose to make a "nest" in a different place. Though this time, I poised the body where I sat for the first ceremony.

The shaman asked if I had a specific wish or intention for this evening—something he didn't often encourage, perhaps on account of the limitations which may arise from a narrow focus. Indeed, Grandmother's expressions had consistently sent "me" far beyond anything I alone could wish for or intend to find.

While meditating in the hours prior to ceremony, I sat with these words:

> "You can't know it, but you can be it,
> At ease in your own life."
> — *Tao Te Ching*

I set this intention: To know without knowing.

Less than 10 minutes after receiving Grandmother's medicine, I felt the need to vomit—this is distinct from purging, which can be described as a release of old energy, thought patterns, and physical ailments often accompanied by vomiting. The shaman often encouraged ceremony guests to suppress vomiting at the beginning of ceremony so as not to evacuate the medicine. He often cited improper diet or dehydration as the cause of this reaction within the stomach. Indeed, I had consumed dairy within the 48-hour fasting period prior to ceremony—a well-known cause of digestive reactions to Ayahuasca.

No longer able to hold it down, I ran across the Alichina Wasi and threw up. Relaxing back into the chair, I acknowledged that the body likely ejected Grandmother's medicine before it could be absorbed by the stomach. I was content to sit quietly in the soft moonlight amongst the other ceremony guests, assuming I wouldn't have much of a journey.

I leaned back and closed the eyes for some length of time, the mouth slightly ajar as the breath returned to gentleness. Behind the eyelids I saw something like a subtle blueish-white haze moving gently, and I opened the eyes. I continued to see this faint haze, which then took a recognizable form in the dark of the Alichina Wasi. It coalesced as the wisping visage of an aged woman, a Grandmotherly figure, standing or hovering slightly above and in front of my seated body, looking at me from a close distance.

This sent a surge of energy up my spine and I gasped aloud. Never had I seen something like this before, nor was I quick to believe what I was seeing. The fleeting form of her textured face, her flowing hair and gentle shoulders, lingered only long enough to recognize her, then again became a light, indistinct, undulating haze. It seemed I had witnessed a glimpse of Grandmother Ayahuasca, the spirit of this sacred plant medicine. Never had I seen through my physical eyes something seemingly non-physical—all visionary aspects of prior journeys were only witnessed with the eyes closed.

Her tenderness, her love, I felt; her patience and understanding was gentle and cleansing. Trust, surrender, and gratitude rang in the mind. Her arms took shape and I watched her hands extend toward me. In them appeared a small rounded cup. Ever-tenderly, she lifted the trough of the cup to feed me.

I choked on the immediate realization that I absolutely had to swallow—whether or not this vision of Grandmother was imaginary, what she poured from her shell-cup was far from imaginary. I coughed the frustrating cough which comes after swallowing a liquid the wrong way, yet no liquid entered my mouth. There was positively no flavor, no viscosity, yet the reaction was there.

I was baffled as this took place. There I sat in a real chair, with eyes wide open, as the hazy apparition of an old indigenous woman appeared to feed me a liquid. Though no tangible liquid was poured, I had to physically swallow in order to inhale the next breath. This seemingly non-physical being very clearly interacted with the physical body, and despite all attempt, the rational mind could not rationalize this. Nonetheless, I felt I was in the best of care.

The mind whirled with questions and I began to see a sort of "tunnel" of concentric hexagons, interspersed with various colors and subtle patterns. I felt an almost violent upwelling from deep within the body, and I knew

I was about to vomit—*"again? How long has it been? What is time, anyway?"* Questions, always questions.

As I hastily stumbled across the Alichina Wasi, the luminous hexagonal patterns obscured my vision almost completely. With each step, their patterns and colors flashed, quaked, and pulsated with increasing severity.

I dropped to the knees amidst this immediate overwhelm, bending over the short, hand-formed clay ledge to purge. With the first heave a small amount of liquid dribbled out, but no physical substance or liquid left the body after this—I had absolutely none left.

I experienced a tremendous reel of memories flying through the inner vision—times of old, experiences I couldn't possibly have remembered of "my own" accord. I saw views of the human self from outside the body while a sort of non-verbal narration played over the montages welling up from inside.

As each memory heaved up and out of the body, I watched it spew from the mouth and into the trees and grass beyond the clay ledge. Not a drop of physical matter came forth. Rather, extensive wafts of opaquely-luminous, nearly iridescent energy left the body.

"The thing is gone," I thought.

I saw the inceptions of fears, moments when I encountered oppositions and childhood bullies. I watched the unfolding of reactions to situations in the past, and I saw how those reactions held tight and continued to replay themselves through various situations over this lifetime. I saw some of the many roots of insecurities, of the hurt child within, of the pains and frustrations of youth, of the relentless cling to the story of an individual identity. I saw all of these things as they flew out, away from the body. For an instant, they vanished from this consciousness.

The 'thing' is the ego. It was laid upon the alter of the Alichina Wasi, as I puked my brain out. Literally, but on a non-physical level.

After a rather arduous half-hour of heaving, the body attempted to rise. I was very quickly humbled, realizing that this had only been the beginning. I was instructed to remain in that spot, kneeling on the hard clay floor until every bit of this release had taken its course.

In the thick of this tumultuous experience, I realized that this purge involved the dissolution of the ego, of the false recognition of "my" self as a separate entity. An isolated, solitary individual I could no longer believe myself to be from this night forth.

To describe all of what was released from this being is nearly impossible. I watched old, tangled messes of emotions, fears, defenses, restrictive thought patterns, mis-conceptualizations and the like expel forth into the trees, leaving the body to seep into Mother Earth. I watched the crackling, luminous energy of these charged emotions and thought-forms integrate into the soil. This energy was usurped through the roots and up into the leaves of the magnificent trees who graciously bore the brunt of this upheaval.

I began to feel powerfully indebted to the Earth for collecting the highly-charged excess I had accumulated within—after all, I had witnessed Mother Earth expel a great mass of indignation from her atmosphere once before. For all of her majesty, I wished I could give Mother

Earth something better than the accumulations of suffering brought on by a myriad of false-perceptions.

Amidst these heaves and musings arose an understanding: every thought, feeling, belief and story purged has a place in the cycle of creation; the release of stagnant energies from the human consciousness provides energetic kindling which Mother Earth uses to feed her powerful creative essence. This decaying energy becomes like compost, or "fuel for Her fire," as it was understood in that moment.

The floodgates of the heart and mind were set open with this recognition. Tremendous forces roared up from deep within until the body lay wasted, exhausted from the great upheaval. After multiple waves and multiple hours of this intensity, eventually, I was able to rise from throbbing red knees and slump back into the chair on the other side of the Alichina Wasi.

As I looked back at the ego/mind identity, I realized the ridiculousness of being caught in it. I began to see the whole limitation, the impaired essence of I. It all became so absolutely clear, simple, and straightforward as it was pondered.

After the massive purging and a time-less moment of contemplation, the eyes closed and I saw beyond the physical realm.

I came into a small, seemingly plain waiting room with four chairs, two facing the other two, backs against the walls.

EGO'S WAITING ROOM

I found myself in a fairly long, narrow room, inhabiting what seemed to be the human body—I didn't question it. The walls and chairs were plain and white. I was aware of a feeling, a mood: it was the feeling of a child's first seating at the adult's table. This distinct feeling gave the impression that arriving here was in some way related to relinquishing the woes of "my" individual identity, to the shedding of ego strongholds, and to the clarity within this state of being. In that moment, I no longer sat at the kids' table—nor was there reason to act from the naive, self-inflicted state of awareness I'd existed within until only moments prior.

There sat three entities, at least one of them displaying very human-like behavior and visual identification. At least one was alien.

I sat in the single empty chair in the waiting room and wondered what I was doing there, what we might be waiting for. Initially, I took the position of not knowing— a mere isolated entity in the presence of others. Then I remembered I could simply ask outwardly the questions I was already asking inwardly.

I felt gentle kindness and a remarkably casual, effortless energy in the beings there. I observed a very alien-looking being seated across from me. This embodiment was of a rather unfamiliar build, not unlike a huge rumpled potato with gristly, uneven skin and odd features. It seemed obvious that this being had sensory perceptions which I did not have, so I asked about them.

Rather than offering an explanation, the being suggested that it would be simpler to briefly occupy the body for a short time in order to directly experience that which

I was curious to understand. I did just that, approaching the being and then effortlessly slipping into the consciousness of the body.

When I jumped inside, I had the intention of experiencing this being's existence or alternate powers.

Upon entering, I "became" his consciousness, but had equally little clue as to what to do with it. Anything that may seem odd to the third person doesn't apply in first person.

The excitement to perhaps see colors I'd never seen or experience a previously unknown form of sensory input quickly dwindled. In taking on the awareness of this body, I could not recognize any sensory input or colors as things "unknown"—for that body, they were very much known, innate, and thus intrinsically part of the awareness within that particular body. I had no outside standpoint from which to recognize any of the bodily processes as "unusual" or "novel". Accepting this, I moved out of the body, and thanked the patient being for allowing this experience.

The being began to explain, whether with verbal communication or otherwise, that the body in use was not "him", nor did it belong to "him" or any particular identity.

Their bodies weren't just impermanent, but borrowed / worn.

The bodies were spontaneously manifested "suits" worn while "on the job", so to speak. They were seated in the waiting room as a sort of courtesy to help usher in those who enter. Otherwise, it was communicated, individual bodies were not inhabited.

EGO'S WAITING ROOM

I asked further, curious about the body-less existence implied to be the true state of these seemingly distinct beings. He explained that they are not truly separate individuals, but that "they" divided into three physical forms to assist individualized beings re-integrate from separateness. Awareness was brought to a door at the opposite end of the room—which was not apparent until that moment—stating that "they" came from the other side of the door, and would return when their work was done. I asked if I could go there too, and in welcoming unison all three bodies said, "of course!"

Their "job" was to hang in this room as a middle-ground between the shedding of self-conscious, mind-identified person-ness and the ethereal truth of the unified spirit of All. The door was opened.

Upon the opening of the door, I instantly recognized what was on the other side: the undulating bands of luminous patterns and colors seen after exiting the Portal to Form.

One at a time, the beings dove head-first through the door with remarkable nonchalance. The warbling strands of color appeared to be the visible surface of a single field—one whole energy. This field did not seem to be contained within anything. It was all-pervasive beyond the doorway.

I watched the entities essentially *become* this warping space as they dove through the doorway—upon contact with the surface, each body simply dissolved or integrated into the field of energy. I was alone in the room for a brief moment, and then dove head-first through the doorway into the warping space.

Mind tried to go, couldn't, got kicked back. I went without it.
HERE I AM.

No comprehension, no brain-based deduction, no ascertainable content was experienced through the doorway. No elapsing of time, no spacial presence or exactness of any kind. I cannot write what it was. I may say that All was within this space. "I" became the whole; the whole simply is "itself." No separateness, no form. No particularization whatsoever, but a certain bounding energy which seemed content, casual, and complete. Here, now. The light of every star and every atom was expressed as a single unitary energy, which was "my" fundamental existence for the flash of presence.

Despite this clear directness devoid of sophistication or formality, a sort of separate presence arose amidst this timeless flash. A form was defined relative to it, that form was called "me," and a vehement attempt to ascertain took over as immediately as it had once dissolved. This presence—the mind—seemed to grab "me" from behind and thrust "me" backward with a violent yank.

This ejection sent consciousness hurling back through the doorway and the physical eyes ripped open once more in the Alichina Wasi, illumined by the moon's soft light. The body was drenched with sweat.

FIRELIGHT CEREMONY I
Vibration & Fractal Dimensions

The evening's ceremony arose to honor a lunar eclipse in communion with *Los Niños de la Luz*—those benevolent energies dwelling in the form of psilocybin cubensis mushrooms.

Prior to ingesting these sacred mushroom bodies, we began with a gentle 30-minute QiGong flow led by our ceremonial guide. This helped open the mind and body by releasing stagnant energy and blockages through intentional breathing and simple body movements, and certainly calmed the rather excitable group of ceremony guests. As we sat in stillness, we welcomed the Children of the Light into our minds, bodies, and spirits by ingesting the mushrooms in present awareness of the movement being enacted. This felt like an immense act of trust and surrender to higher energies, to the vast realm of the unknown and unknowable.

Each of the 12 ceremony guests was given a candle and invited to set a personal intention. One by one, we lit our wicks from a single flame held by the ceremony facilitator, symbolically "igniting" the intention imbued upon each candle. We offered our candles to light the central fire, which was set upon a large, low stone alter built and engraved with the geometry of the Incan Cross. As the wood began to morph into the living light and heat of a fire, embers rose up and out of the circular opening in the center of the roof above.

"Each spark is like a messenger, holding the capacity to carry our intentions, questions, and energy out to the world and into the depths of the universe beyond. You may enact this."

"May I become the light," the voice whispered as the eyes followed an ember lofting into the moonlit sky beyond.

The voice of a trickling stream sang with living energy as it flowed through the roots of the coastal cloud forest. From this stream, water was diverted into a small heated pond and mixed with the oils of *palo santo* and lavender—this is where I now sat listening to the multifaceted voices of existence.

I wheeled around at the deep boom of a drum to face a man dressed in a native mask and a large feathered headdress, standing tall and extraordinarily still, save for the motion of his arm pounding the heartbeat of this large, resonant drum. After this fragment of eternity, he set the drum next to the heated pond and I immediately felt a compulsion to play it. This was sensed, and the drum was placed in my hands.

The drum takes me to a dimension beyond.

Something beyond "me" wanted to play. This "something" watched as the body stood up, carefully slid the drum's hand-sewn strap over the shoulder, and breathed a few breaths.

With the eyes closed, a very clear image of a man's torso arose directly above the body. To describe this, one could say his image came into the mind's eye, and spatial awareness of his presence was felt standing or floating above the head. This being had the face and bust of a Quechua elder, dressed simply, without elaborate headdress or feathers. Upon the feeling of fascination and humble welcoming, this spirit drifted into the crown of the head, assimilated into the body, and began to play the drum. I watched the arm and hand gently move the mallet as feet began to move precisely and rhythmically around the warm pond.

The drum's deep tone began gently, spaciously, and intensified with each pulse. The rhythm was, at first, that of a sacred heartbeat. This gradually deepened and spontaneously broke into divergent rhythmic pulses beyond description. These asides did not follow any standardized rhythm, but felt essential to this movement—the body and footsteps followed seamlessly with no conscious thought of "my" own.

This Native spirit was felt rather powerfully throughout the body and began to transmit energy into the group of people seated in the warm pond, who had fallen absolutely silent as the body danced in circles around the quaking water. Energetic ripples flowed across the stone ground with each footstep, and each beat of the drum sent waves of colored light pulsating through the vast depth of night, enveloped by the moonlit canopy listening high above our heads. A voice I'd never heard began to chant and sing through me.

A distinct feeling was communicated while this unfolded. The elder spirit expressed true elation to play the drum—like a person reunited with the passion of a lifetime.

"We so rarely have a chance to play. Few spaces are opened for us to play the drum anymore." These words came with an energy which seemed to refer to the abandonment of traditional communion with ancestral spirits. Where this was once a common and intentional practice, now this spirit was left to pursue any possible opening he may find. One is left to wonder if the ingestion of psilocybin and the willing embrace of benevolent energies in some way helped the body receive this ancestral spirit. Or, perhaps it was nothing more than the play of imagination.

Eventually the spirit's pulse of the drum gently faded to silence. The body was flushed with a sense of contentment as this spontaneous expression closed. The drum was gently placed upon the Earth with gratitude.

I awoke to what could be called the fourth dimension. This started as an awareness of different "neighborhoods" existing amidst each person; dwelling places, towns, so much to potentially explore within this shared conscious space. All is connected, sharing, becoming, teeming with life! My consciousness had the chance to move through this unseen "space" without reference to the body.

This brought about very potent observations which left a distinct impression as to how life experiences are built or stored up within the individual consciousness. I seemed to move through visual reproductions or symbolic representations of the psyches of each person around the fire, which blended into one-another as I navigated through sprawling person-hoods. Each was extraordinarily different, and each came with its myriad of feelings. I walked the roads of mental constructs, perhaps observing places, people, and scenes stored in the memory of each individual. The level of detail, depth and subtlety of these scenes far surpassed the extent of experience and capacity contained within "my" mind.

While exploring one woman's mental suburbs, I passed an antiquated restaurant with a neon sign, of which a few letters were unlit. I entered houses and ran through sunlit fields, stood beneath looming skyscrapers and dove into intimately known relationships—some of this felt painfully gloomy, some luminous, some dull and uneventful. All were foreign or unknown to my individual memory, though the sentiment expressed through each scene, experience, and relationship was wholly present while moving through them. I was aware of the dynamic shifts in tone, scenery, and expression as I intentionally flowed around the ceremonial fire from one person to the next—these seemingly distinct physical and psychological dimensions were interwoven. As awareness moved through physical space around the ceremonial fire, so too did it move through this psychic space.

As the connotations of these movements became increasingly obvious, I could no longer dissuade myself from acknowledging the reality of that which was being perceived—this in itself would have required me to delude or ignore that which was made immanently evident. Thus, I felt I was directly violating the privacy of others—both strangers and friends—and shifted the energy beyond these individual facades and vistas.

This eventually unfolded into a space which I could witness from every angle simultaneously, inside and outside. This place was not unlike the Tower of Piza or Tower of Babel.

I explored unknown worlds, so far outside my mind's scope that there's no sense in recalling. But it exists in consciousness, forever. All of time is now, here.

I recognized how people could "slip away" so to speak, not returning to the dense, perhaps far less stimulating, human form.

I hope never to forget the unfathomable laughter which overtook my ability to do anything else while we all crammed into the warm pond. We sat knee-to-knee, putting sound bowls on our heads and staring into the infinite depth of the dark water. Ripples, wiggles and wild noises, frequencies of wonder and true bliss on Earth. We could all literally see the colorful ripples of energy rippling off the bowls, moving through water and air. Vibrations. Life is an absolute miracle.

All came to life... the true state of creative hallucinations. All of the Earth, everyone, the whole thing is an incredible masterpiece of wonder.

In all reality, the energetic movements were so intermingled, we all laughed as one. All truly is one, and we tapped into it with extraordinary laughter.

I felt as though my laughter became everyone else's. A point also arose when everyone seemed to gather around me, while this collectively channeled and interconnected energy was strongest. I truly felt my presence not just in everyone, but as everyone. As I laughed, I was Tito laughing. I was the mallet hitting the bowls.

We closed the night watching smoldering ashes come to life, the beat of a drum and harmonica, tibetan bowls, and chants pouring forth through me like I'd lived with the Seminole Natives.

"Become the light" was my intention. Alignments are occurring. Clarity dwells where ego-self-identity once reigned and pillaged. Grateful, grateful, grateful for All. It's a wiggly world!!!

JOURNEY SIX
Informal Operation

What a precious, precious gift. Tonight's Aya ceremony found me in a rather relaxed, focused state. As the gentleman next to me began to throw up, [mother shaman] sang the sweetest Icaros... "venga, venga, por aqui, venga venga por favor... venga venga en puro, venga venga corazon..."

I began to intensify my breathing, as I felt Grandmother's spirit with us. [the shamaness] reminded us at the beginning that 50% is the spirit and higher power / guidance, 50% is our own responsibility. Tonight, I began commanding, with respect.

A few verbal cues:
"____ is this?"
"Why am I here? (Earth)"
"Breath me; become, become, become."

As the energy flowed in, I felt a presence lifting my arms, which were now zizzling, teeming with energy.

Sitting quietly and completely still, the arms were lifted with no point of contact. I wondered if the shaman walked over and started doing unusual things, but no physical presence was responsible for lifting my otherwise limp arms; no person, no hand, no object, no thing touched the body other than the chair I sat in. Yet, there I observed the arms, moving around above the head and spreading into strange positions.

My hands wadded up. This presence guided my arms up and around, held out to the sides, head and chest up and open. Rotated down, hands to the floor, couple cycles with a periodic electrical burst throughout the body.

This felt like an operation, of sorts. Eventually the arms were spread out slightly behind the body and out to the sides. The head was pushed back, the chest very much exposed and open. What became clear during this drawn-out process: Because I agreed to allow this to happen, I surrendered a level of choice in the matter. When I attempted to move the arms back to a more comfortable position, this was strongly resisted—I could choose to move them freely, but there was a very real opposing energy to this attempted movement; the sort of opposition one might expect from a dentist to a squirming patient mid-procedure. I heeded this, resting in a peculiar amazement, wondering at the dynamics of this interactive, yet seemingly intangible, presence.

Whatever occurred here, whatever sort of operation was being conducted, whatever gave rise to this, I know not entirely.

INFORMAL OPERATION

My hands hung near my feet for quite a time. Old energy drained from my toes, hands, arms, legs.

Imagine the inner space of the body completely filled by or immersed in a liquid of sorts, like a bathtub. Seated in a chair, the torso is slumped over the thighs and the arms hang down toward the floor, chin nested between the knees. Now imagine the "water level" within the body beginning to slowly descend as it flows out of the bottom of the feet, emptying first the neck, shoulders, chest, torso, elbows, hips, knees—like a bathtub draining. After perhaps 10-15 minutes of this, the last ounces of liquid dribble slowly out of the feet and hands. The remnants drip down the interior surfaces of the body like honey melting down the inner surface of a jar, the shallow pools of remaining liquid at the base of the feet patiently draining out. These were the palpable physical sensations experienced in the body.

I cried, in such a way. Overwhelming gratitude as I asked the beings responsible for overseeing this energy surgery for guidance. "What's this for? Why am I here?"

I dropped to child's pose as my hands became moderately more functional, energy seeping from Third Eye to Pachamama. Thank you.

I was instructed, non-verbally, to sit on the knees and lay the forehead on the ground. I attempted to uncurl the wadded, locked-up hands so as to place the palms on the cool clay floor of the Alichina Wasi. This time, I felt this "liquid" sensation seeping out of the head and face through the center of the brow. Again, I felt a very clear "water-line" slowly descending inside the head and face as it drained out and into Earth.

I had the clear understanding that what drained from the body was a sort of energetic goo which had coagulated within the body over the course of this lifetime. With it went various tensions, densities, dead memories, and the like. Gracious gratitude filled the body as this energetic cleanse unfolded.

I rose into new clarity, knowing without knowing, and sat in the seat. Leaned. Starting with the brow, then to the ears, heart, organs, and so on less clearly, Grandmother cleaned, cleansed, got rid of all unnecessary junk. I felt this, nearly saw it. Down to my very core. As this gently faded—thank you— I looked to the shamaness, defocalized, and saw all sorts of wild, amazing features, entities, personas, I don't know. Powers.

A ceremony guest saw my energy field as purple: "transmutation."

INTERLUDE
Unlimited Energy

Life looks, pouring forth, through 'my' eyes. I am it, as are the wings to a butterfly.

If the body "receives" non-local consciousness in a way similar to a smartphone receiving satellite data, then the ego, or isolated self-identification, can be likened to the operating system within the phone. As soon as a phone's functionality is limited to that which only it can, itself, produce, alike to being set to "airplane mode," its scope of operation is narrowed considerably.

The phone's inability to wholly function without this connection, despite having all the internal components necessary, is equivalent to a person who is stuck within the operational capacity of the individual ego, shut-off from a broader connection to the energetic source of aliveness. The flow of mana, prana, qi, ki beating the heart and breathing the breath is an essential aspect of this connection—it is an aspect of the resilience of life-energy.

The fracture formed by the concept of an 'I' which does not draw from and necessarily decry the very facts of existence is preposterous. Though, this is the backdrop we paint for ourselves; the identity, ego; part of the whole. But indeed "part" and "whole" go together like the wing and the butterfly. They give way to the paradox, to the illusion of perceived reality—the screen, the interface, the radio without a signal.

Awareness was brought to the importance of one's connection to the source of life, to the broader context of aliveness which I am, which we are, which moves through every body. This energy seems not to arise directly from the physicality of any one individual body, but is essentially the aliveness which lives through the body—the energetic consciousness seeing through every eye, photosynthesizing through every leaf. This energy is universally present—it is presence. By embodying or perhaps "reconnecting" to this fundamental energy we may fuel and energize the human body in seemingly extraordinary ways, many of which are only veiled by the ignorance of modern humankind.

An example: the morning after ceremony, I went for a sunrise swim in the ocean. On the walk back I harvested a hearty rack of wild-growing bananas to share at our post-ceremony integration circle.

One obstacle stood in the way: returning to the Alichina Wasi required a hike up the steep 350-foot-high coastal cliff upon which it sat. Though the mildest grade of the cliff is rudimentarily paved, only 6-cylinder vehicles can climb it. Even on sunny days, 4-cylinder vehicles inevitably and precariously roll back down the hill. Hiking up empty-handed was demanding in itself, so to carry this heavy rack of bananas up the cliff seemed quite a challenge. By the time I considered this, I was already walking up the hill.

I began to observe the body from the perspective of the presence operating through the body, not of the body. "I am not the car, I am the driver of the car," I thought.

UNLIMITED ENERGY

The words, "unlimited energy; you are unlimited energy," arose through the mind, looping like a mantra. I observed the mind giving complex streams of instructions to the muscles, organs, circulatory system via electrical impulses. The lungs acted as powerful pressure-engines, expanding and flooding the body with air and vital energy. Pores poured like miniature overflowing dams, setting free body heat and toxins while cooling the skin. Streams of energy pumped down through the hips, thighs, shins and feet, grounding into the Earth as if the legs were lightening rods.

The whole body operated as a unified system, a symphony of incalculable layers of synchronized rhythms and melodies. I watched this occur from a vantage of detachment. The body hiked itself up the hill, carrying the awareness I am just as it carried the rack of bananas. I made no effort, I did not feel strain, I did not experience the tiring of muscles—it was complete fluidity of motion, unobstructed flowing energy.

Though effort was exerted by the body, this felt entirely effortless of the body—the energy was not sourced from the body's own reservoirs, but flowed through the body. As such, there was no depletion of energy within the body whatsoever. Upon reaching the crest of the hill where I'd typically stop to cool down, the body did not need to stop to rest or catch the breath. The body was entirely at ease, and continued on to the Alichina Wasi.

Confidence, child. It's not "you" working here. It's the whole of existence which you simply are. The palm, racing clouds, dancing breeze, the salt in the ocean, the color of the eye.

The work here-now is syncopation: of the degrees of consciousness, of fractal zones or planes of existence. Merge? Or explore?

JOURNEY SEVEN
A Vision, A Dream

A practice of Quechua shamanism lesser-known to Western Culture is the ingestion of a tea made from the leaves of the Tobacco plant.

Despite the global commercialization and manipulation of this plant, potent varieties of naturally-occurring Tobacco have grown throughout El Oriente for millennia. Tobacco continues to occupy a fundamental role in the medicinal therapies and spiritual practices of indigenous peoples throughout the web of humankind. Indeed, Tobacco is considered by some to be the mother of medicines, often superseding Ayahuasca in importance and profundity in its medicinal affect on human consciousness.

One form of therapy starts by pouring a handful of Tobacco tea into the palm of the hand. One then lifts the cupped hand to the face, rocks the head back, and sharply inhales the liquid up the nose. This is a powerful cleansing agent which liberates the sinuses of congestion and dryness. A feeling of warmth often surges across the forehead and scalp upon the first inhale, giving way to cool relief of the mind and body.

A more significant preparation and ceremony follows when three or more ounces of this potent Tobacco tea are ingested orally.

Upon reaching the stomach, this Tobacco medicine enters the bloodstream and begins to systematically detoxify cells with which it comes in contact. This happens by a sort of "door-to-door" process, as the Tobacco molecule is highly effective at permeating cell membranes throughout the body, binding to and removing numerous toxins and damaged cell matter from within. Much of this is dumped into the bloodstream to be processed by the excretory organs and expelled, which often happens through any and all available orifices. The high concentration of toxins all sweeping through the bloodstream at once can feel quite painful and uncomfortable.

Beyond the physically medicinal qualities of this practice, drinking a large quantity of Tobacco tea may induce visions, and often presents journeys which may seem similar to those witnessed with Grandmother Ayahuasca.

Pre-Ceremony:
I invite fear to kindly leave the mind, body, and all other aspects of being.
I invite clarity in. I let go of "I"-dentity.
The whole is greater than the sum...
Thank you, ally spirit.
Trust, surrender, gratitude.

Roughly 6 oz. Tobacco tea to drink after 3 inhales and a teaspoon for the stomach.

I sat upright, well aware of wakefulness as the inner vision opened and arose.

I crawled and bounded through thick tangles of softly luminescent "vines". These didn't appear to be made of an organic substance—certainly not one I am aware of. Their luminosity most closely resembled that of an exceedingly bright purple-blue glow worm.

We move through weaves and weaves of tangled wood, roots, vines, medicine energy. Searching.
People seeking "me", they showed the way to "me". Tumbling.
"He is a healer with a medicine that is sweet."

The shaman, shamaness, and my mother accompanied me within this vision quest. We were searching for something in particular—a medicine which I was intended to become familiar with in some way. Within the journey, the only communication I received about this medicine was that it is "sweet"; whether of taste or of some other quality, I cannot say for sure.

I went to bed and, after a couple hours of churning and aching discomfort, the overwhelmed body dropped into sleep. I soon arose in a dream.

Strangely, this dream was a continuation of the vision which began earlier in the evening while in ceremony—a distinct quality of Tobacco which I have not experienced on any other occasion.

Morphing colors bubbled up from a warbly ripple which I moved into, or that swallowed me whole. More than one arose, but I only recall moving into one, into a snowy landscape in search of... the medicine.

This entrance into the dream-vision was very clear.

Visualize the surface of still water, so that it occupies the full field of inner vision. Now imagine rain beginning to fall on the surface of the water, creating radiant concentric ripples. Watch as these ripples form not just concentric circles, but irregular, curvy ripples. These ripples then begin to carry out in three dimensions, moving in loose, warbling "spheres" toward the point of observation and in all directions.

See these colorful concentric warbles morph into various portal entrances, which ripple open effortlessly. Volition to move through these undulating portals is present. One portal in particular seems intriguing, or otherwise draws the attention in toward it. Intentionally entering through the wiggling portal, awareness flows into the space beyond the threshold of the portal.

I found myself in a snowy, hilly landscape, with a few trees standing above a thin layer of soft powder. The shaman, his wife, and my mother were again present, continuing to insist that I find a particular medicine. There seemed to be an urgency, as if others were waiting for us to return, perhaps hoping that I'd find the medicine for some treatment. I climbed tree after tree looking amidst the barren branches, but found nothing in particular.

As I sat perched in a tree, an immediate and nearly violent upwelling roared from the body's depths and awareness was thrust out of the dream.

Vomit, 3AM.

JOURNEY EIGHT
Fear, Myself, & I

To some degree, Grandmother Aya taunted me last night.
She clearly exposed my fears, and the attachment that I've formed to them. While in the Alichina Wasi, a tarantula, cockroaches, and multiple other bugs found their way onto my arm, into my hair, etc. The night was incredibly dark but I felt the creatures when I grabbed them and threw them off.
Fear cripples me on more nuanced and far more significant levels than that of my proximity to giant bugs.
Even in my own casita, here, away from most humans, where millions of birds are currently singing loud and free, I'm afraid to sing for the fact that someone might hear me sing poorly. This is an astoundingly resolute insecurity toward what is perhaps the most enjoyable or liberating form of expression I know. I'm so identified with this deep-rooted insecurity that I give myself no possible room to sing beautifully.
I just recalled a dream in which I was in a city (something like Boston) and was in a huge, 6-story labyrinthian college with all kinds of strange lad-

ders and halls. Somehow I'd been led away and ended up in the city, lost, and asking for directions. In this process I ended up naked, and eventually I got back to the college through a large grassy field.

I was searching for a particular room on the highest floor, but couldn't find it. I became uneasy, almost frantic.

Why have I had so many different dreams of large structures in which I can't find my way up to a particular place on a particular floor? Why is the structure almost always unoccupied, or if so, soon evacuated? What do I seek in these spaces, or do I even ever consider that question?

WHEREIN LIES THE ILLUSION CALLED FEAR?

Fear is attachment to "I", an obsession. A refusal to let go. An overprotectivity of a false ego. Defense. Deep insecurity. Identification with the products of the human. Uncertainty of outcomes. Avoidance. Wariness of foreign contact (giant bugs). Attempt to avoid harm, ridicule, etc. A need for acceptance but the refusal to allow it in.

Fear feeds upon itself, thus the death of the manifestations of this illusion means the death of the illusory body of fear—the death of these enmeshed symptoms of reaction in the reproductive cycle of fear's falsity. Fear doesn't exist beyond ego identification and the attachment to particular outcomes or states of existence, which are perceived to be ideal or complete or "finally good enough" to the identified mind.

Yet, I am absolutely crippled by this illusion of fear. I won't sing publicly, I won't share what wells up in me, I won't heal, I won't truly GO—not until I've eradicated the fear which casts such a tremendous shadow upon this one consciousness.

But aye, fear of fear is fear, itself. Tricky bastard! It turns "against" itself to feed itself at last resort. I see you operating within me now. The spotlight has exposed you, as much to show that you really aren't "there" at all. You're a phony. You don't exist.
You don't exist because "you" are "me", and "I" don't exist. Leave the ego and it ALL falls away. Fear is a lie "I" have told myself. An elaborate story.
THE END.

Fear manifests as obsessive avoidance. It's a phantom of imaginary constructs. It's the structure in which no staircase leads to where I'm going—dead ends. In this, it's attachment to going somewhere in particular—also illusion. The compulsion to arrive, to go elsewhere, either bred from fear or... well, a manifestation thereof.
It truly is reactionary. "This, so that."
I'm coming to find that "I" wallow in fear, and thus, ego.
I-llusion. Ill-usion. Dissolution.

Moreover, the fears which cling most strongly are internal-force fears. Though the external forces (to use dualistic terms) do play a part, ultimately I fear the internal interpretation of my own self-worth, or lack thereof. How ridiculous.

Say, for example, someone who dislikes [an accomplished musician] also happens to dislike my vocal expressions. Rather than allowing that person's preferences in music to exist for him/her, my typical reaction would be one of self-pity, insecurity, etc.

On the contrary, I have very little reservation when boarding a flight to an unknown or little-known land. In this I have confidence; not just in "myself," but in trusting the forces of the world which have proven themselves to be not only trustworthy, but intrinsically "part" of "my" consciousness, the totality of consciousness unfolding synchronistically.

For these movements, by and large, "I" step out of the way so that the fullness of being can presently unfold without obstruction. What a polarity to the internal fear-hell "I" has concocted. This has deep roots in the assumption of separateness, in the illusory mis-understanding that there is any difference whatsoever in the movements and energies which flow inside or outside. What is different is the extent to which "I" obstructs this energy's free movement and expression through the humanic vessel, with which "I" has become so falsely associated. It's EGO.

So then, what does the transmutation of this ego-fear-ridden identification look like? How might, how must, "I" bring about the end of this illusory state of being?

> "Can you cleanse your inner vision,
> until you see nothing but the light?"
> — *Tao Te Ching*

After integration, it's clear that fear and ego are one. Identify with ego, fear things.

Though, this is psychological fear. Biological fear is one of the great motivating forces on Earth; the great adrenaline-flooded actions that occur, the gazelle fleeing the cheetah.

The shaman spoke of the art of battle, like martial arts. The biological fear which rises can bring us to the next tier, push us past the threshold of what we think we can do, or think is possible.

The shamaness asked, in relation to insecurities and fear of expression:

"For whom or for what are you doing it?
To whom or to what do you look for value or acceptance?
Whom are you attempting to please?"

This very simply dispels the fear. Also, the shaman showed that fear can't exist if we are present. Interpretations like fear arise from thought, have anchors in the past or future.

It's just THIS: THE-IS.

FIRELIGHT CEREMONY II
Listening

Life is never short of fascinating. Another wonderful, wiggly ceremony at the ceremony space. Seventeen people this time, including my mother and I. The intention I set was: "listen."

Listening is typically understood sonically, but the rising energy within the body played with all of the senses—I listened with each in turn: ears, eyes, nose, skin, through feelings/mood, etc. Though, one form of listening kept turning off: linguistic. I hardly payed attention to the Spanish flowing around me.

I hardly spoke at all. It was actually quite amazing, allowing the whole of life which is outside of human interaction to come, alive. Even my mind quieted for most of it. Simply resting in awareness.
The moon was full and the air was cool outside the fire area. Staring at the moon, clouds danced with impossible textures and movements. All the natural sounds, the tree limbs leading to heaven's night, the cosmos within the warm pond water; I really felt the vastness of worlds unfolding around our skin, in the tiny dancing particles and water of the night.

Others were pulled into this presence and, I think, got to taste some of it. People from the city who rarely stop.

Part of this listening was, perhaps, non-reactivity. However, some of this attentive listening happened in a way which also held notes of fear, or lack of action.

For example, the drum—I just don't like having to "perform". The expectation of performance is a huge turn-off. As soon as it becomes performance it ceases to be true, and is thus dead in a larger sense; however exciting or colorful it may be on the outside, it's within the matrix's game.

This is all bringing to rise a realization. One which goes past these situations, toward a larger whole.

The realm of human-based action, the standpoint of only existing within these very narrow confines, is what I ultimately listened beyond for nearly the entire night. I was even aware of this while drumming; we need not add noise to the amazingness in which we have yet to truly bask to begin with. What a marvel, non-active listening. I'm seeing now that this requires immense restraint, immense non-grasping and non-reactivity. In a way, too, this passivity can be an escape as much as an exercise; a balance is necessary. There's a more expansive existence beyond these human relations, and I was very overcome by these aspects of reality last night.

How can this awareness unfold through 'me'? What might this be, this reality? What unfolds when "I" is truly let go?

Ah! 'I' belongs to, and perhaps even gives rise to, "the world of 10,000 things," as stated in the Tao—the world of never-ending reflections and shadows, of the dance of wonders and the ultimately illusory nature of their permanence; of the voids, of the compensations we attempt to fill and fulfill. The pure unquenchable joy we often long for, consciously or unconsciously, is so ironically hidden, covered up, by this shadow play.

By attempting, by acting in order to glimpse it, we give it up. We trade it away for fleeting follies. I rested in the Great Foundation last night, the ground-floor of pure joy which comes not from futile attempts, no outward motive, but which belies all of this; the space in which the Many can be is the pure essence which Is.

We find this, we intrinsically become this, upon truly listening—through senses, through inner awareness, through breath, in stillness.

This allows for total fluidity, for fun and great freedom from human triviality in the spiritual inquiries. This is a grand opportunity to do not-doing, to deepen into this wholeness. To be the finger pointing to the whole cosmos, as the cosmos, fundamentally.

> "Because he has given up helping,
> He is people's greatest help.
> True words seem paradoxical."
> — *Tao Te Ching*

JOURNEY NINE
The Ocean

"Everyone must walk to the ocean."

The shaman spoke these simple words as we sat alone in the stillness of night. He continued in metaphorical prose, speaking of the journey of Earthly life in terms of a river's journey to the ocean. Mid-stream, he promptly informed me that I hadn't yet left the Alichina Wasi.

Perhaps fifteen minutes had passed since I received Grandmother's medicine, and I was ready to resign to the now-familiar space of a still body and an empty mind. Nonetheless, with a gentle sweep of the shaman's rattle I stepped from the cool clay floor of the Alichina Wasi. Reverberations of the ocean's voice cascaded up the steep river valley, and I began to walk.

This was the only Journey for which I physically left the container of ceremony. I carried a journal, a pen, and a small jar of Tobacco tea. With no more than a faint sliver of moonlight I could see with ease—I counted the leaves of the towering canopy as I bounded down the cliffside toward the expansive ocean.

Life moves of its accord. I stand in the fluid motion, vibratory undulations warping about my static feet. Every motion is so brilliantly alive, so fully, wholly itself. No words can contain the direct experience of uncontrollable energy, life's essence unfolding in real conscious awareness, and the perfection and essentiality of every gurgle, every ripple.

A dog walks briskly, greeting kindly and carrying on, pointing a nose toward the river outlet where I would return.

A finger points to the moon; the moon reflects the light of the sun; the sun...? Reflections, shadows, the thing itself, the essence which belies all... "The Golden Thread".

This life really is a dance of reflections. Light bounces around, fills the eyes, transmits signals which compress the info into such rudimentary slivers of the wholeness that it's amazing we're able to do anything at all. Or perhaps we don't.

To sense, to know, is to reduce. We pick the tomato from the vine, pulverize, and cook the soup to our liking, thus destroying the real, or its representation.

And fear is the silliest (no)thing of all! "Fear" in a biological sense is survival, a curious mechanism. Psychological fear often departs from survival and deals in the quality of survival, whether socially, economically, or the like. It nit-picks and rules our days, keeps the car safely between the lines, stopping well ahead of the white line when a cop is present. Fear curtails our wandering, builds our walls of illusion. Fear robs the present reality, turning it into a false sentence, unjust and ultimately unsupported by anything real.

Fear is a clap in a vacuum.

Firelight Ceremony III
What Shines the Sun

Wild-foraged mushrooms made for an energetic evening. The ceremony space was upbeat and talkative, so the strong pull to leave the body became rather subdued/grounded.

"Scrub the launch."

In turn, the body was inundated with the presence of energy, internally. The body vibrated like in qigong but kept going, the dan tian area near the navel and in the gut felt like a densely coagulating ball of heat and vibratory energy. This had a yellow/orange/white feeling, which in writing makes sense considering solar/sacral area.

Rather than consciousness rising away from the physical body toward some experience or otherness, energy amalgamated within the body and flowed through the human vessel.

If the body was a radio through which a powerful tone was being transmitted, the abdomen was the internal speaker-cone vibrating in order to emit the tone outwardly.

At will, this energy could be moved throughout the body, so I experimented with intentionally conducting it through the hands. When I did this, I saw waves of energy rippling out from a point near the center of each palm. The energy ebbed and flowed with the inhale and exhale.

I recognized the potential to cultivate and direct this energy occupying me, so a close friend and I went to another room. We meditated, and then a series of energetic surges began. I knew I had to share this, to direct it. What followed was immense.

She lay flat on her back and I placed hands above her heart, as one would when facilitating Reiki or QiGong healing (practices in which qi-energy is drawn through the body and directed out of the hands with benevolent/healing intention). She was a trained Reiki practitioner. I was not yet trained, but I had received Reiki treatments from friends and was generally familiar with the practice. We were both open and willing to experiment with energy in this unfolding moment, as we both felt a strong energetic field emerging.

As I breathed huge breaths, a channel opened and I truly felt the pump-action between breath and energy. Surged in powerfully.
These words and others spoke through me, as much to me as to her, to whom they were directed:

"Know your power, feel it. Be the power—you are this power. What beats the heart shines the sun. The light of the sun is here. You're filling with light. Not later, right now."

Physically, my arms rippled and quaked. It was as though every atom grew 10x larger, every muscle expanded to near bursting as energy poured into the crown and out of the hands, into her. I felt/called in the power of the Sun.

This was so powerful and unlimited that I consciously capped my intake, for her and my own sake.

She shook almost violently as an energy capable of hurling 50 cars simultaneously shook me to the very core of life essence.

We both cried healing tears between heaves of highly-charged emotional energy which arose from the depths. Amidst these apexes of sheer intensity—which felt like electrical heat pouring through the body—nothing was harmful or painful. The ability to consciously direct this energy felt as innate as the aliveness of the body despite the lack of formal training on the human level.

I inhaled to coalesce the energy as the hands moved up and away from her body. With the exhale, hands moved toward her body and energy poured forth through them. With the eyes closed, I felt the energy flow through paths in her body which looked like tree roots to the mind's eye. It was clear that her body had a threshold of capacity—that space would have to be made to continue filling with this energy. So, with her permission I attempted to remove excess energy from the body.

If she was a French press, my hands became the mesh screen which "catches" and separates the dense coffee grounds. In this way, the hands began to function like a filter, pushing and sweeping energetic blockages and density from the crown of her head out through her feet to be returned to Mother Earth. This process cleansed and purged the energy in her body to increasing fineness.

I saw and briefly felt the presence of thick, sticky, black "goo" as it was collected and removed. I simultaneously felt this occurring within my body, though it was directed toward her body.

I observed carefully as these movements took place. I witnessed and learned about the dynamics of living energy and one's ability to mutually guide it through a willing body. I recognized a sympathetic relationship between the bodies—where an imbalance was detected within her body, I became aware of it via a temporary sensation in that area of the my body. As energy was intentionally focused in these areas of her body, I felt the imbalance shift or resolve within this sympathetic dynamic. In this way, our bodies became mirrors, reflections of one body with only the appearance of separateness.

Curiously, the whole process felt like a symbolic representation. I was filled with a recognition that what appears to be a physical body is essentially a visible map of one's energy; the body is perhaps a representation and physical manifestation of the energy of one's consciousness, one's being.

This expanded the context of physicality, health and physical injury, pain and healing. I considered the physical injuries I've experienced, and that these may be expressions of energetic dynamics rather than arbitrary happenstance alone. Indeed, acne is commonly understood as a physical manifestation of the energy of stress. Perhaps this could be extrapolated to acute injuries, chronic pain, sickness, and the many other variables and conditions of the physical body.

The health of the physical body is perhaps indicative of the clarity of the energy of the spirit. To balance and heal the energy, to clarify the manifestation of the indwelling aliveness, is to heal the physical body by proxy.

JOURNEY TEN
Grandmother's Blessing

I dove into the beating heart. The mind was still and calm. Each yawn seemed to push me through dimensional thresholds, through warmly colored spaces, fractals flitting about. Each space became more serene, still, gentle, like the womb; floating.

I went into various spiral vortex / whirlpools of energy, seemingly to emerge elsewhere, but I was distracted by some strange sights: saw a snake with mouth open, super up-close. Became it! Slithered with incalculable speed and ease.

After that, I came to a crystal-like pyramid floating in space with a transparent goldfish hue. Some wild technology? I rose up into it through the square bottom, but 'saw' nothing upon entry. Hmm...

I then stood upon a luminous ribbon-like pathway wafting through indistinct, vibrant spaciousness. A form coagulated of no-thing—first, long strands of flowing hair arose, then a light blueish-white dress which was filled by a human-like female body. Her face was not of static identity; the features shifted and morphed with unquestionable fluidity. Perhaps the most stable aspect observed was the joyously casual, easefully ecstatic essence embodied in this feminine form. That energy—call it love—seemed the very basis or foundation of this being, now approaching. She graciously and non-verbally communicated her role as Grandmother Ayahuasca.

I met Grandmother! I began to ask questions after greatly thanking her for all of the immense unfolding she has incited in this life. I considered the recognitions from a previous ceremony: that no matter what, I'm here on Earth. Why am I 'here'?

Grandmother held my hand and we began to 'walk', prancing. She giggled and teased me; I kept asking, "why am I 'here', on Earth?"

"How badly do you want to know?" She poked and prodded, stirring and riling me up.

"I want to know!"

This series of questioning seemed brief and interminable. With all due respect, some part of "me" still insisted upon a resolute answer. Her lovingly teaseful responses plucked the weeds of deduction and reason from the garden of spirit within. We held hands and skipped through spaciousness along the warbling ribbon-path for vast, timeless eons.

I reflected upon the great upheavals Grandmother helped incite within the spirit I am. I felt empty spaciousness where thick, sticky, dark "goo" once festered. A lingering uncertainty drifted along, an energy which sought guidance in cultivating this garden of spirit. It was clear that one's choices ultimately determine what grows in this garden, and the gravity of this responsibility felt immense—like jumping from a precipice of infinite potentiality.

"You're here to wonder why you're here," she said, laughing.

The cosmic joke! Grandmother made it clear, in this simple statement, that the question to be wondered hasn't much of a linear, brain-based answer, but instead, the question itself will lead me through the life I'm here to live. It's about asking, about the process itself, rather than some kind of neatly-packaged answer; answers are insufficient shortcuts—obnoxious, sweeping generalizations.

Don't bother seeking answers, simply ask the questions and go for the ride. Adventure into the depths and see what's going on. Share these adventures, open the doors, bring the wonders into the light; bring 'others' into the light of the wonders.

How can I bring some of Grandmother's wisdom back? I asked her authority: may I write and share her teachings?

"Yes! YES!"

Grandmother's elated enthusiasm to my writing was so inspiring, and relieving! She wants to be shared, and she trusts the lens through which I see—so very much has been sculpted by her.

Thank you, sweet loving being.

Integration

One may neither anticipate nor directly pursue awareness of a cosmic nature; just as one may neither anticipate nor directly pursue a color one's eye cannot see.

For this, the expansion of perception is key. With tremendous willingness and surrender, one may cleanse the lens of perception to peer through an open aperture unfiltered. By releasing all constraints of thought, identification, physicality, and spirituality, one may integrate the underlying essence of *cosmos* into oneself by way of the spontaneous journey. Within this is the amalgamation of *cosmos* and *chaos*—for, true to the paradox of life, both are facets of one integral whole.

I am profoundly grateful for the presence, guidance, and friendship of the shamans throughout these journeys, and for the vastness which is not to be written. Above all else, emphasis is placed upon integration. To "integrate" is to become one, to unite and re-unite with the essence of that which may appear separate. The extent of one's experiences in this human life, the profundity of a realization, the expansiveness of any journey may be determined by its integration into living reality. Without intentionally weaving a seemingly profound experience into the fabric of the life within which it exists, it may be no more profound than a mosquito bite.

In these writings I have shared the initial, immediate expressions of each Journey. Now five Earth-years after the first of these Journeys, they are as clear in awareness as they were the very evening they unfolded—they are living energy, ever-expanding as they continue to be woven through the fabric of this existence, like water coursing through the myriad morphing landscapes of daily life.

Through the winds of time, innumerable layers of integration have given way to many challenges and confusions on the human level. As the integral essence I am dismantles and burns away attachments, identifications, relationships, comforts, lifestyles, joys, sorrows and everything in-between, the individual ego-consciousness often feels powerless—especially where it once ran rampant. This process of integration endlessly strips the ego to the core.

Nonetheless, one both requires and inherently embodies the gift of individuality in this human realm. Perhaps the subtlety is in identification. To be identified as the individual ego, to perceive one's aliveness as the individuality alone, undermines the totality of Self.

Can one's finger point without the existence of the hand, arm, body, brain? Can a tree live without the existence of soil, water, minerals, microorganisms? Does the aliveness of Earth exist of Earth individually, of its own terrestrial influence alone, or is a radiant star also fundamental to the existence of Earth life? Could Earth and Sun exist without the existence of space and the structure of physicality?

Simply, that which appears to exist individually would not exist without the existence in which it exists. From this vantage, perhaps neither the chicken nor the egg came first. Perhaps one's individual aliveness is funda-

INTEGRATION

mentally rooted in that which is prior to and beyond the individual alone—as such, physical reality may be seen as the fundamental "body" in which the many individual parts have their being. One may say that every individual fundamentally is the integral aliveness of existence, even when conceptually isolated and fractured by a rigid identification with individuality. As such, choice and identification are what they are, aspects of One whole in kaleidoscopic expression.

The shaman often referred to the capital letter "I" as a symbol comprised of two horizontal lines connected by a vertical line: this may be seen as a representation of the seemingly distinct "planes" of Oneness and individuality connected through the upright vessel of the human body. The I, oneself, is this unity in conscious expression. Simply by being, one is Life, living.

May the integral essence shine indiscriminately through All, One.

www.ingramcontent.com/pod-product-compliance
Lightning Source LLC
Chambersburg PA
CBHW020909080526
44589CB00011B/511